My Travels
Around the World

NAWAL EL SAADAWI

My Travels Around the World

translated by Shirley Eber

Methuen

First published in Great Britain 1991
by Methuen London, Michelin House, 81 Fulham Road, London SW3 6RB

Copyright © 1991 Nawal el Saadawi
The author has asserted her moral rights
Translation copyright © 1991 Shirley Eber

A CIP catalogue record for this book
is available from the British Library
ISBN 0 413 17460 3

Photoset by Rowland Phototypesetting Ltd
Bury St Edmunds, Suffolk
Printed in Great Britain by
St Edmundsbury Press Ltd, Bury St Edmunds, Suffolk

Contents

To all who travel
and who know exile
far from the homeland.
And to all who know exile
in the homeland.

Nawal el Saadawi

Introduction

I wrote this book, *My Travels Around the World*, before 1984 but it was not published until 1986, in Cairo. All my works are written in Arabic and I try to publish them in Cairo first. If this fails, I try to publish them abroad. At the time of Sadat, I used to publish in Beirut because of the implicit or explicit censorship of publishing.

In the era of Mubarak there is no censorship of books and I am not on the black list as I was during Sadat's time, but I *am* on the grey list because I'm one of those who prefer freedom of expression to the approval of rulers and the powerful.

Nowadays, the media are under government control, and most of the critics are employees whose wages are paid by state institutions. For this reason, they are only interested in books which interest the state.

Thus, in Egypt, the attention given by the media to most books is superficial or is paid for by the powerful, or has no discussion of thorny issues related to political or religious restrictions or to anything concerning women and their liberation.

Sadat gave the green light to extremist Islamic trends, which have been given the name 'fundamentalist', to strike at the other political forces that oppose him. Thus, the power of forces hostile to liberation in general and to women's liberation in particular, was strengthened, and attacks on and hostility to women increased.

Naturally, I felt the climate of hostility during the seventies and eighties (and until today), to the extent that the government placed an armed guard before the door of my house in al-Giza for almost two years (1987–1989), though I never knew exactly who it was that threatened me with death.

I travelled to many countries of the world and wrote much about my travels, of which – due to publishing restrictions – I have only published little, but I was able to publish this book which contains accounts of some of my journeys, my first trip by plane, some of my dreams and childhood memories.

Travel has many aspects, since we see other countries and other peoples, but the most important aspect of travelling is that we are able to learn more about ourselves through seeing others. We see our homeland more clearly when we are away from it than when we are in it. I have seen many positives and negatives in the East and the West, which have revealed to me the positives and negatives within my own homeland.

This book contains my travels during the sixties and seventies. As for my travels during the eighties they will be included in the as yet unpublished second part of this book. This first part of my travels represents the initial pulse and my new feelings when – for the first time – I stepped beyond the borders of my homeland.

It is a book that is dear to me, even if it does not contain everything I wanted to say and, like other of my writings, has been subject to the censor's scissors or publishing difficulties and restrictions.

History repeats itself. In August 1964 while I was in the United States, Lyndon Johnson was talking of peace, then sending his soldiers with weapons to Vietnam.

Now, in August 1990, I hear George Bush talking of peace – as I write this introduction – and sending his troops to Saudi Arabia to start the Gulf War. Yesterday I noticed on the front page of *al-Ahram* newspaper (Cairo, 19 August 1990) the photograph of the American aircraft carrier *Eisenhower* and an American warship crossing the Suez Canal, bound for the Gulf in readiness for war.

I turned the page to find a photo of President Bush fishing at his summer residence, then one of Margaret Thatcher spending a pleasant holiday with her husband by her side . . . Whilst American and British forces were preparing to ignite the fires of war in the Arabian Gulf for one reason: Kuwaiti and Saudi petrol.

Writing this introduction I cannot ignore the spectre of the destructive war which hovers above our heads and those of our children, for no other reason than that some kings and rulers of our Arab countries are simply functionaries of the American administration. It is the logic of armed force that rules, not the logic of justice, and the aggression of the Iraqi president is no more offensive than the aggression of the American president!

Were it not for the American and European military protection given to these kings and rulers of our Arab countries, not one of them would remain on his throne; but the fall of these kings and rulers means the loss of American and European profits from Arab petrol. And who pays the price of the American military arsenal which takes up its position in the Arabian Gulf? It is the kings and rulers of the Gulf states, primarily Saudi Arabia, who are paying billions of dollars for retaining their thrones and their opulent lifestyles whilst millions of Arab people go hungry: one son of the Saudi King Fahd lost thirteen million dollars in one week on the gambling tables in Paris, according to Western news agencies, and as reported on the front page of the Arab press (*al-Ahali*, 22 August 1990).

How much we have read about the wealth which these Arab princes and kings squander in the bars and brothels of Paris or London or New York or elsewhere! Enough to eliminate hunger and disease and backwardness in the Arab east and west. Petrol money goes into American and European banks and into purchasing American and European arms which are useless. Why does Saudi Arabia buy American weapons at the cost of billions every year and then find itself incapable of defending itself and have to ask the American army for help and protection when threatened?

I have only been to Saudi Arabia once, more than ten years ago, when I was working at the United Nations and had a blue passport which allowed me to enter many countries without a visa. I saw for myself the extremes of backwardness and subjugation in which the Saudi people, men and women, live under the shadow of this regime. In Jeddah I went into a bookshop and asked the assistant, 'Have you any of Nawal el Saadawi's books?' The man replied, 'No, madam. They are banned here . . .'

I heard from some young Saudi women that they had obtained several of my books from this bookshop. I wandered around among the bookshelves and bought a couple of Islamic publications that were on display. As I was paying for them I asked the assistant, 'Do you know that I am Nawal el Saadawi?' He examined me for a moment, then smiled and said, 'No, I didn't know, but now I remember having seen your photo in some Beiruti newspapers.'

The assistant and I engaged in a friendly conversation over a cup of coffee. He told me about the strict censorship of books, that my books were absolutely forbidden, but that sometimes on request he smuggled some of my writings from Beirut to Jeddah.

He reached down to a concealed shelf and took out some of my works that had been published in Beirut. He told me about the Saudi regime and the torture meted out to those who oppose it in the prisons. He said, 'Prisons here are not like your prisons in Egypt, Doctor. Our prisons are underground pits and those who enter seldom come out again.'

Such is the dictatorial, patriarchal class-dominated regime of Saudi Arabia, protected by an American regime which claims to be the protector of democracy and human rights all over the world. But double standards rule the world, East and West, and for this reason no one believes the tears of sadness shed by countries, particularly America, for the rights of the Kuwaiti people invaded by the Iraqi army. Every day we read about the children, men and women of the Palistinian people in the occupied territories, whose blood is spilled at the hands of the Israeli army. How many times has the United Nations called for the imposition of sanctions against the state of Israel or South Africa for their violation of international law or the international court of justice or the resolutions of the Security Council – and still these sanctions have not been implemented.

And yet, today, America and Britain (and other major industrialised countries) are rushing to intensify sanctions against the Iraqi regime over and above those called for by the UN, even to the point of imposing hunger on the Iraqi people by a naval blockade or death under the threat of war in the Arabian Gulf!

I only went to Iraq once, many years ago, and I believe that the Iraqi people suffer the same terror under Saddam Hussein's regime as that suffered by Syrian people or Saudi people under their own dictatorial terrorist regimes.

Some of my writings are banned from entering Iraq, in the same way that they are forbidden in Egypt or Kuwait or other Arab countries. I visited Kuwait ten years ago or more and delivered a lecture on Arab women, after which I was forbidden entry again, simply because I had given such a lecture which was violently attacked in the press in Bahrain.

Readers who have read those of my works that are translated into English, such as *The Hidden Face of Eve*, will realise that I do not separate the liberation of women from the liberation of people or from the oppression of local and international patriarchal class systems. This will be clear in *My Travels Around the World*.

Nawal el Saadawi, Cairo
August 1990

PART ONE

First Trip
Outside
the Homeland

In childhood, the homeland was love. My mother's warm breast. The smell of milk. My father's hand on a cold night covering me. My grandmother's voice on summer evenings telling tales of monster and sea sprite. The aroma of bread and cress and cactus fruit. The jug on my cousin Fatima's head, brimful with water of the Nile. The waves of the sea at Alexandria. And the roar of students in the streets shouting: Down with the King!

In my youth, the homeland became revolution and revolution was love. Now love was forbidden, revolution too became forbidden, leading me to prison rather than to freedom.

My life's dream was flight and escape from prison. In my childhood, I had a recurrent dream: my father was dead and I started going out without permission. In my youth, I had another but similar dream: my husband was dead and I came of age.

My father was the greatest love of my life, and yet I envied children who had no fathers. The first revolution in my life was against my father – he wanted to marry me to a man I did not love. With the fantasy of adolescence, I lived in daydreams. In fantasy, I loved a hero who bore arms, smote enemies and freed the homeland, then held me in his arms and kissed me till I swooned and forgot father, mother, sisters, brothers and grandmother, and all my pain.

But when he *did* hold and kiss me, I did not swoon. Neither did I forget anything, not even my grandmother's tales of monsters, genies and spirits. I discovered the first facts of life: that first love is an illusion, heroism is fantasy, and the homeland is not liberated.

3

In the middle of the night, I crept out of bed. The sound of snoring was loud; his mouth open, over his top lip a thick black moustache. On tiptoe I opened the door and went out. I walked rapidly, almost running. I had only one goal: for my mother to wrap her arms around me. I stopped suddenly, when I remembered that my mother was dead and that she had never once in her life embraced me. My father too was dead, without ever having embraced me; neither me nor any of my brothers and sisters.

I'd be away at boarding school for the whole academic year. Then I'd come home, but no one would embrace me or kiss me. In our house, kisses did not mean love. Love was just deep feelings, deeply buried. Not words or embraces or kisses but silent love, expressionless and motionless, except in fantasy.

It was the tragedy of my life; reality is always less than fantasy. My life became one continuous attempt to realise my fantasy and dreams. And what was the dream of my life?

I saw myself on a white stallion, flying through the air, in my hand a sword with which I felled the enemy and liberated the homeland. I had been born in a country ruled by foreigners. My grandmother gasped when I told her about my dream:
— That's no dream for girls.
— What do girls dream of then, grandmother?
— Of bridegrooms and wedding dresses.

But I dreamed neither of bridegrooms nor of wedding dresses. Still, my grandmother bought me a wedding dress ten years before the bridegroom came.

Every holiday, my father bought me a new dress and my brother a gun and small aeroplane with a spring which you wound up to make it fly. In the yellow cardboard box lay my present: a silky white dress with ruffles on the bodice and lace on the sleeves. I shouted angrily: I want a plane and a gun like my brother:
— You'll be beautiful in the new dress, my mother said.
— I don't like dresses, I yelled.
— That girl should have been a boy, my grandmother shouted.

Despite my grandmother, I would look up at the sky with the eyes of a ten-year-old. Would a day come when I'd fly in an aeroplane? Could I fly through the air like a bird, far away from this prison into which I had been born?

In dreams, I would fly without an aeroplane. My body lifted into the air and I circled above the rooftops and trees and seas. Then, suddenly, my body would plummet earthwards and plunge to the bottom of the sea.

– Flying in dreams means success. You'll marry a king or the son of a king, my grandmother said.

– I hate the king, I hate marriage, I would shout at her.

– As crazy as your mother, she would say, flapping her hand angrily.

My mother hated King Farouq, but my grandmother hated only the English and used to sing along with the radio:

> *King of the country, oh so wise,*
> *King Farouq, apple of my eyes.*

I can hear the sound of my new black shoes on the floor of the airport as if it were yesterday. Twenty years have passed since I first saw an aeroplane on the ground. It looked bigger than I'd imagined. In the sky, it looked as small as my brother's, the one with the spring.

I stood in the queue, before and behind me foreign men and women, expensive leather cases in their hands, wool coats over their arms, heads held high, backs stiff, tall in stature.

I raised my head and straightened my back. I was as tall as any one of these men, and the women were shorter than me, their skin chalky white, their eyes yellow discs, their mouths lipless lines moving rapidly when they talk, like taut instrument strings or whips.

In the washroom mirror, I saw myself wearing the black raincoat I bought from *Omar Effendi* shop after getting my exit permit from the passport office in Tahrir Square. I was holding a new black bag with a shoulder strap, and sticking from its outer pocket was the tip of a green passport, a long red ticket and a square yellow immunisation card.

Through the wide glass window I could see the planes on the tarmac, like huge hunting birds or mythical reptiles. The roaring of take-off and landing rang in my ears, ran through my body like a shiver, a mixture of terror and joy and courage and fear and obscure sadness. It reminded me of my wedding night and of the night my father died.

In the mirror, my eyes sparkled with an intense black light, my skin brown and flushed with enthusiasm. The door of the aeroplane before me opened onto the wide world.

The policeman sitting at the entrance to the airport stopped me and asked for my papers. I handed him the yellow paper with the stamp of the eagle, the symbol of the state. The policeman examined the yellow paper, making sure the eagle stamp was real and not forged, that the state agreed to the transfer of my body beyond the borders of the homeland.

What has the state got to do with the movement of my body?

The policeman moved his eyes from the yellow paper to my face. Then slowly from my face to my photograph glued onto a bit of cardboard. My face did not look like the photo. He did not see the momentary sparkle of hatred that glinted in my eyes as I looked at him. He did not know that between policemen and myself there existed a three-thousand-year-old enmity, stemming from the time the god Amoun dominated and destroyed the civilisation of Isis and slavery came into existence.

Staring into my face with narrow eyes, the thick moustache on his upper lip quivered, reminding me of the snoring that came from beneath another large black moustache.

– This is the authorisation of the state. But where's her husband's? I heard him say.

I stared at him in surprise. Dictatorship may mean that the state controls my whereabouts. But husband? Does he, too, govern the movement of my body? What's the dividing line between being state property and husband's property? My eyes clouded but then I suddenly realised I was not married. The mist cleared and my voice rang through the airport hall like a silver bell:

– I have full jurisdiction. Nobody governs me other than the state.

– I'm asking for your husband's authorisation, the policeman snorted gruffly.

– And I'm telling you that according to the law, I can travel without a husband's authorisation because I'm a free woman, without a husband.

6

– Have you got anything to prove you're not married? he shouted angrily.

I snatched out of my bag a long piece of paper that looked like a birth or graduation certificate. I held it over my head like a flag or lifebuoy. With another quick movement, I placed it in his hands.

He brought it up to a police magnifying glass and examined it closely. He checked the stamp, the authorised signatures and the witnesses, then snorted:

– Why didn't you tell me from the start that you've been divorced?

– I haven't *been* divorced, I replied angrily. I *am* divorced.

Although twenty years have passed since that first trip abroad, my voice still rings in my ears as I stress the word *am*. The policeman sitting in front of me behind a metal enclosure stares at me with narrow, half-closed eyes, like those of an imprisoned animal. I can still recall the movement of his hand as he raised it and brought down the black stamp like an iron hammer on my passport and let me pass.

At first, I could not believe he had let me pass. Slowly I walked ahead, thinking that he'd stop me. But he didn't. I took some more steps, a little less cautiously, and still he did not stop me. Joy and surprise overcame me: I leapt across the borders of the homeland as though reborn, clapped my hands like a child and moved across the ground as if about to soar off into the air, my face skyward, my back towards the homeland. On the aeroplane steps, I looked back, imagining a policeman was following me and that at the last moment he'd stop me. Then the doors closed and the steps were removed. Through the round glass window, I saw the observation balcony; hands were raised and waving. Not one of them waved to me. Many faces, but not of them one that I knew.

I turned my head with the plane as it taxied away from the airport buildings and my eyes clouded over. Through the mist, my daughter's face appeared, her small hand waving, tears in her honey-coloured eyes. I went up to her to kiss her and take her hand firmly in mine.

Pain just under the ribs, deep, and heavy as lead. A piece of myself was still there, in that small apartment – her skin was the same colour as mine, her fingers looked like mine. I imagine her crawling on hands and knees; she looks wide-eyed towards my bedroom and does not find me. I tensed my body as if to get up and go back, as a sudden surge of maternal feeling in the form of passionate longing swamped my joy at travelling. The homeland waved to me from afar, like a child's round face, eyes filled with tears; five delicate fingers which wrap themselves around mine on contact, like a stake fixing me to the homeland, like a root burrowing into the earth, I had become like a mother tree when I had not yet outlived my own childhood. My mother-hood and my childhood both lived within me in mutual contra-diction. My longing for my daughter was as contradictory as my longing for the homeland, the desire to belong only equalled by the desire to escape.

My fingertips trembled as I felt the seatbelt, the aeroplane roared as it began to take off; then suddenly I was separated from the ground, lifting into the air, the beat of my heart rising and rising. The plane shook as if about to fall. Then the beating under my ribs subsided. Beside me, a man was reading a foreign newspaper as if he were sitting at home. He had a long curved nose, reddish-white skin, and was wearing a multi-coloured tie; his fingers holding the newspaper were white, the nails carefully manicured.

Through the round glass window, the yellow sands stretched on and on. Houses receded and shrank and the River Nile was a thin white thread, its banks two black ribbons; then the desert like a sea of sand, sprawling on the horizon.

For the first time, I saw my homeland from afar. It had grown small, a mere line twisting like a narrow snake in an expanse of desert. Everything in my life receded: my joy and my long-ing, my motherhood and my childhood, my hopes and my dreams. Everything had shrunk. Even Abdel Nasser and his thundering voice and the rows of statesmen quaking before him had become a mere line at the bottom of the page of a foreign newspaper held by the fingers of a foreign man.

I had believed that my homeland was the whole world, just as when I was a child I believed that our street was the whole homeland. As I grew up so the street grew smaller. But when my being reached out beyond the homeland, the earth shrank and new feelings, that I was larger than before, filled me.

Through the window, the wings of the plane kept their shape and size, fixed, motionless and suspended in space above waves of steady white clouds. Nothing in the universe moved, not the clouds, not the plane, not even the tea in the cup placed on the white plastic table hanging on the back of the seat in front of me.

I stared fixedly hour after hour; it is then I discovered that travelling by train was more enjoyable, if only for the movement I would see from the train window. Telegraph poles and trees would run backward so fast the eye couldn't catch them, filling me with the movement of life as I sped towards my goal, the blood racing in my veins at the same speed, emotions flooding with happiness. Since childhood, travel had all the joy of a feast day. For it, I'd put on new clothes and new shoes. I'd not sleep from happiness and get up before the dawn call to prayer or the cock's crow. Travel, then, was by car or train and within the homeland, from Cairo to our village of Kufr Tahla or to Manouf or Alexandria or al-Giza or to wherever the Ministry of Education wanted to transfer my father.

My brothers and I would race to sit by the window. My brother was a year older than me but I'd beat him to it. My little brother, though, would cry and cling to the window, so I'd leave him the seat. My sisters were younger than me and the youngest one sat on my mother's lap.

I knew nothing about aeroplanes other than the distant hum I heard in the sky and a small body that glinted on the horizon, the size of a dove, whose movement was as slow as a cloud. My imagination was unable to conceive its true size or speed. I could not imagine how normal-sized human beings could fit inside it, looking down on us like gods from above the clouds. My imagination did not extend to picturing myself inside an aeroplane in the sky looking down on the universe from a tremendous height. My imagination extended horizontally with the movement of the car or the train on the tracks or my feet, and the reach of the Nile at ground level.

When I raised my head vertically towards the sky, the eyes

of those around me became alarmed, particularly my grandmother's. From the time I was born, she looked anxiously at my
raised head. Should I have been born without a head? If I
stretched my neck, her anxiety increased and she'd shout: don't
lift your head like that! Can't you see how proper girls walk?

Proper girls walked with their heads bowed. Till the day she
died, my grandmother kept on saying that I wasn't proper.
That was my grandmother Amna, my mother's mother. But
grandmother Mabrouka, my father's mother, would place a tall
clay jar on my head and say: don't bend your neck like that!
See how the village girls walk with heads high. But she believed
that girls' heads were only held upright like that in order to
carry clay jars on them.

I loved grandmother Mabrouka more than grandmother
Amina and I preferred to travel to her mud house with its
wooden veranda and drink from the water jug and bathe from
the water of the Nile although my mother preferred going to her
own mother's house in Cairo. My father, like me, loved to
spend the summer holiday in his mother's house in the village.
My parents argued about it at the start of every summer holiday
but it was never a bitter argument and it ended with neither of
them winning. There was a sort of balance between the great
powers in the house: one time my mother would pack the bags
and we'd travel to her family, another time to my father's family
and so on.

A few days before travelling, I'd take all my clothes out of
the wardrobe and pack them into a large suitcase. My mother
would come and empty the suitcase into the wardrobe, shouting: don't take all your clothes. Anyway, it's not time to go
yet!

She would stand on a high wooden chair and on tiptoe reach
up to put the case on top of the wardrobe. From where I stood
looking up, I could see her fat, white and hairless calves stretching up under her silky robe to even fatter and whiter thighs,
then coming together at the end in one deep dark line. A strange
thought would come to me: that I had dropped into the world
from this dark line. This was immediately followed by an even
stranger thought: that my father too had a connection with this
dark line. Here my thoughts stopped completely, as if I'd

reached the end of the world. I returned to earth, then clambered onto the high wooden chair and reached up to the top of the cupboard, but I could not get to the suitcase.

Every night, from the start of the summer holidays, I would dream that my arm grew longer and longer and grasped the suitcase, that all my clothes were moved from the cupboard to the case, that my mother was waking me at dawn to put on my new clothes – my father made sure the windows and doors were locked, the taxi waited outside. The sound of the engine buzzed strangely in my ears and the smell of petrol in my nose intoxicated.

At the train station, everything seemed amazing: the high platform, the tracks running endlessly in a deep trench, the sounds of bells and the whistles of trains, the thick smoke billowing from black funnels, the people running with cases in their hands, the samit seller calling out loud, the steep steps of the train. I would grasp the metal rail and put one foot on the step, imagining that the train would move off while my other foot was still on the ground. But the train did not move and I would run to my seat and look out of the window. The station and the houses stayed still and I was just thinking that the train would never move when suddenly my head was thrown violently backwards then forwards, the houses began retreating, followed by the telegraph poles that started running after each other, one by one.

I put my head out of the window, sobbing for joy. The wind made my hair fly, my wide-open mouth gulped in the air and the smoke as I felt my father's hand pulling me back. His voice rings in my ear, mixed with the noise of the train wheels: put your head in!

I pulled my head back from the window. But I'm inside an aeroplane, not a train and the window is small and round and locked by double glass. The sky is a constant blue, the clouds a constant white. There are no moving trees or telegraph poles and I can't put my head out of the window. Neither can my body feel any movement. It's as if I'm in a closed tin can. The seat belt around my body ends in a metal lock. Its touch on my chest is like a doctor's stethoscope dangling on rubber tubes round my neck. Behind me, an old man is coughing. His cough is dry, from smoking, not from tuberculosis. My ears are attuned to identifying diseases from the type of cough.

Every day, from eight in the morning until two in the afternoon, I would listen to the coughing of the long queue. I put a metal earpiece between jutting ribs and listen to the whistle of air, to the rush of blood and pus. I bring the X-ray machine down onto the chest, saying to the patient: hold still. And instead of holding still, he coughs into my face, showering me with spittle. I step back quickly and press a bottle of medication into the veined hand, saying: one tablet, three times a day, after every meal.

The voice, weak with wheezing, repeats: After every meal?

– Yes, I say, after every meal. Three tablets per day, after three meals!

The question comes in gasps: Three meals?

– Yes, three meals, I repeat.

One day, at the end of the queue was a woman, one child in her hand, another on her shoulder: Would I be sick with tuberculosis if I ate three meals a day? she raged.

Every day, staring out of my window onto the brackish pool, I would look up at the small patch of sky between the walls and address God: who is responsible for such misery on earth? You or the head of state?

I held the head of state responsible and not God, for I still believed in divine justice.

One day the telephone rang suddenly, making me jump. I imagined that the security department in the ministry had picked up my deep-seated doubts in the justice of state as a voice with a cultured accent came through: A ministerial decision about your travelling in the doctors' delegation to Algeria has been made.

With every trip abroad, I thought, I will not return. But I did, every time. My longing for my daughter drew me home together with my longing for the land, the smell of the earth and the soil and the air, the familiar faces and features. My ears craved the language and the accent of home, a craving which was a sharp pain in my ears, in the heart under my ribs, in the movement of blood in my veins; like the craving of an addict for the pain of poison.

I stared from the window at the earth of the homeland. The face of the security official was still before me, his bald head shining like that of a turtle, his eyes two white lenses without lids or lashes. He had examined me from head to toe and my whole being turned into a shrimp glued under the lens of a microscope, apparatus like an X-ray machine revealing what was inside me. I hid the hatred deep within and drew over my face saintly features full of love and fear. For nothing threatens security like hatred or love without fear.

It was the first time that I had stood for examination before a security official, to get that small rectangular booklet called 'a passport'. It was the first time in my life that I had owned a passport. With the passport safely in my handbag, I walked along the street, head held high in pride, as though with this booklet I had climbed up a rung. But the pride soon dissipated, as the huge administrative building of *Mugama' Tahrir* swallowed me up and my body fell into a pit crammed with panting, sweaty bodies. I too began panting as I ran from office to office, in my hand papers stuck with stamps of green and yellow and signatures of red, black and blue. Finally, I ended up in the security office. The clerk looked like any other clerk – bald head and soft voice. He looked me up and down, stared at the photo of my face, then asked me: Why are you travelling to Algeria?
– To attend the Arab Doctors' Conference, I said.
– Are you a doctor? he asked, as though surprised.
– Yes, I replied.
Looking into my face, he said:
– What do you think of the revolution?
– Which revolution? I asked.
But understanding the question, I then said: Yes.
– Yes? he said.
I started to think.
– What are you thinking about? the man scolded angrily.
– About the answer, I said.
– Does the question need thinking about? he asked, surprised.
At that moment, thinking seemed to me to be something

shameful. The meeting ended quickly. I spent a month waiting to get an exit visa, but the visa did not appear.

Tuesday came. The following day, Wednesday, was the travel date. I went to the security clerk and asked:

– Why is my visa late?

– It's always late, he replied.

– Isn't there a way to speed it up? I have to travel tomorrow.

– No way to speed anything up, he answered.

I returned home. The walls of the apartment were closing around me. I put out my hand to the telephone as the ringing of the bell echoed in my ears. No one in the world, I am completely alone. I went to the window to look out at the people in the street. A smell like the overflow of a sewer filled the air and the wind carried dust and heat. People moved in the street like dead ghosts from another world. A police wagon with a piercing siren towed a car behind it. Violet feelings of alienation surged through my body.

A red bus pulled up. My daughter jumped from it, wearing a blue tunic with a white collar, satchel in hand. She looked up at the window and saw me. She smiled, her eyes glowing with joy. I ran to the door and waited till she'd come out of the lift, then took her in my arms. She buried her head in my chest. The smell of childhood in her hair awakened my maternalism and dispelled my alienation.

I prepared food for her and sat watching her eat with relish. My whole being focused on that plate toward which she put out her small hand, which she raised to her mouth, the movement of her small jaws as she chewed the food with pleasure.

That night I slept with my arms around her, as if embracing the whole world. Nothing in the world afforded me such gratification, no man or work or travel. My imagination that night was still. One picture dominated my mind: that the plane had fallen into the sea with me in it. My disillusion with travel turned into joy at being saved from death and I fell into a deep sleep.

In the morning when I opened my eyes all my desire for travel had completely vanished. I went to the hospital like any other day, but the telephone rang beside me and the cultured voice said: Your visa has arrived.

14

I put the phone back on the hook. Security permits, it seems, do not come when people want them, but when they stop wanting them, they suddenly come from who knows where, like fate and divine decree.

I awoke to a voice coming from the ceiling of the place announcing that we were circling over Libya. My body was slumped into the seat, a delicious torpor running through my being. I had crossed the borders of the homeland. I rested my head against the back of the seat, closed my eyes, then opened them. There was music in my ears and a pair of blue eyes looking at me, smiling. A woman was sitting in the seat next to mine, holding a large plastic doll in her arms, rocking it as if it were a living child.

– Have you got any children? she asked me.

– Yes, I said.

– I can't have children, she said sadly.

– There are things in life other than children, I said.

– Like what? she asked.

– Work, travel, love . . . I replied.

– Have you ever been in love? she asked.

The question surprised me. Nobody had ever asked me such a thing before. But her question seemed normal. I had a desire to open my heart to this woman who did not know me; we would part and not meet after today.

– Do you want to know the truth? I said.

– Yes, she replied.

– I've had the illusion of love, but I haven't loved yet, I said.

She laughed, throwing back her thick blonde hair. I noticed a gold tooth in her upper jaw. Her nails were long, manicured and painted red. She took a lock of her hair between her fingers, licked her top lip with the tip of her tongue and said:

– There's no such thing as love.

– Where are you from? I asked her.

– I'm Italian. I work in Benghazi.

– What do you do? I asked.

– I'm a dancer, she said, lighting up a cigarette. Then, her voice lowered, she continued:

– And a prostitute.

With an almost instinctive movement I recoiled from her. It was the first time I'd met a prostitute. I'd only read about them in novels and seen them in movies. From the corner of my eye, I studied her features, her arms, her legs. Everything about her was normal, unremarkable. I had thought that prostitutes must be remarkable in some way. I stared at the five fingers of her hand in surprise, as though expecting her to have six or seven. Suddenly I came to with a violent shake, as if the plane had fallen into the sea and my stomach with it. Clutching the seat with both hands, I shouted: What's happening?

The Italian woman said: We're landing at Benghazi.

A rectangular panel of light lit up above my head. English lettering read: *Fasten seat belts. Extinguish cigarettes.* A female voice announced over the intercom that the plane was landing; I didn't hear the rest because the microphone swallowed up half the words and the deafening roar the other half. The walls of my ears stuck together and closed up under a sudden pressure. All I could hear was a piercing whine. Then suddenly my ears opened with a pop, the pressure vanished completely and I heard what sounded like the roar of a waterfall. My body was shaken with the thump of the wheels of the plane as they touched the ground.

My face must have been ashen because my heart was pounding and my throat completely dry.

Through the window, I saw her on the tarmac of Benghazi Airport, walking in line, one slender white arm carrying the plastic doll as if it were her only daughter, her other hand holding a yellow leather case.

A gust of sand blew, making her blonde hair fly and I saw her cover her white shoulders with the edge of her shawl. But the Benghazi wind defeated her and lifted the shawl off her shoulders. Brown faces ravished her, hungry eyes devoured her.

I saw her stop, then turn towards my window. She waved to me from the distance with a small white handkerchief and I waved to her with my hand, a curious apprehension running through my being.

*

When we landed in Algeria the warm late afternoon sun shone above the towering green mountains and trees. For the first time in my life, I saw a mountain rising towards the disc of the sun. In Egypt, I have seen only flat land. *Jabal al-Muqattam* is not a real mountain, and the green in Egypt is not this deep, intense colour.

Behind me a voice said: *hamdillah ala as-Sallama* – thank God for your safe arrival. I turned to see a long brown face, a neat, decorative moustache on its upper lip. His name was Dr Jamil Yasser, and he was a professor of mine at college.

– Are you alone? he asked.

– Yes, I said.

– Come with us, he said. We'll take a taxi to the hotel.

His wife was with him, a large fat woman tottering on spiky high heels. The Algerian driver spoke in French. My wrist-watch showed 8.30 but the sun was still in the sky.

Dr Jamil Yasser said: Haven't you changed your watch? It's 5.30 pm.

I turned the hands of my watch back three whole turns.

Despite my numerous trips around the world during the last twenty years and although I have turned the hands of my watch backwards or forwards many times, I still remember that first time I changed time with my own hands. I had thought that the movement of my watch was inviolable, untouchable, unchangeable. Those hands governed my waking and my sleeping, my work time and my pleasure time. They ruled the days of my life, during my youth or my adulthood. Not I myself, nor anyone else, not even the person who had made them and shaped them into hands, could move them backward or forward by one minute. But these two inviolate hands I could now move back three whole turns.

Surprise changed to joy, as if I had pilfered three hours from the gods and added them to my life . . . or as if I had gone around the globe three times while standing in the same place.

As I walked on Algerian soil, the sun still in the sky, I said to myself: the sun has set for people in Egypt, but it's still in *my* eyes. Is it the same sun or another one?

The Algerian accent seemed to me like a new language, the Algerian features strong, sharp and as lofty as a mountain. The people's national anthem, when I heard it played for the first time, reminded me that I was on Algerian land, the land of a million martyrs; the war of liberation and *fedayeen*; prisons of torture and *Jamila Buhareed*; French soldiers and the atrocities of colonialism; Franz Fanon and his book *The Wretched of the Earth;* Ben Bella with his round face and tall stature, like that of Abdel Nasser.

Ben Bella opened the medical conference. The *Ibn Khaldoun* hall was full of Arab doctors. They talked of the Algerian revolution, of sacrificial work, of liberation from colonialism. But soon they divided into specialised committees and began talking about diseases of the heart, stomach and spleen.

In the evening, there was music, song and Algerian dancing. Words and tunes on the piano mixed with the beat of tambourine and *'oud* (lute), French words with Arabic; I saw eyes in which were revolution and anger; eyes in which were resignation and satisfaction; elegant, semi-naked women; women with heads and faces covered under heavy veils, their cloaks wide and white.

In the Arab *qasba* quarter the beating of the tambourine and the *'oud* dominated the piano and the words, Arabic dominated French. The humid alleyways, the old dilapidated houses, the eyes of women from under their white *hijab*, the wan faces of the children. A woman came towards me, her face and body hidden under a cloak, a child on one arm, the other one stretched out to me, palm up:

– Give me a piastre, she said in French. It was the first time I had heard anyone begging in French. I thought beggars knew only Arabic.

I returned to my hotel room before midnight, to find a piece of paper – neat decorative words like the neat decorative moustache, one letter lying beside the next, like one hair lying beside the next, so neat, it's like an notice: *I invite you to dine with me tomorrow. Jamil Ali.*

I hardly recognised the name. Was it Dr Jamil Yasser? I had attended some of his lectures in the *Ali Ibrahim* auditorium in the medical faculty of *Qasr al-'Ain*. He had delivered a talk at the conference the previous day on a new method of removing brain tumours. He was of medium height and stocky, especially round the middle and thighs. In conference halls I had seen him walking with his wife, a few steps in front of her.

In the morning, the telephone in my room rang:
– This is Jamil, a voice said.
– Jamil who?
– Dr Jamil Yasser.
– But on the note you wrote 'Jamil Ali'.
– My names are Jamil Ali Yasser.
– Then why didn't you write Jamil Yasser?
– I was worried in case someone else found the note.
– Do you mean that 'Jamil Ali' is a pseudonym?
– Something like that.
– And why disguise yourself?
– Traditions make us, wherever we travel.
– Are you against traditions?
– When I travel, yes.
– Is your wife coming with you?

He was silent for a moment, then said: No. She prefers staying in the hotel. Shall I pick you up at six thirty?
– No, I said.
– Are you turning down my invitation?
– No, I'm turning down the invitation of Jamil Ali.
– Why?
– Because I don't know him.
– And Jamil Yasser's invitation? he asked. Would you accept it?
– No.
– Why?
– Because I *do* know him!

From Algeria I took the plane to Paris. Flying no longer held its initial magic. Through the double window I saw the Straits of Gibraltar, the strip of sea between the continents of Africa and Europe.

The word Europe filled my head with fantasies. The first time I had heard it was from my father. I was still a child when I heard him say that outstanding students went to Europe to do their research. I thought my father was better than any man in the world, that nobody could be more outstanding than he. When I grew up a little, I discovered that King Farouq was more renowned than my father. I asked my grandmother why my father had not become king. As I grew up still more, my father decreased further in stature. Then I learned that there were men who had travelled to Europe to do their research and he had not. My father died at sixty-one years of age without having seen Europe, without having taken a plane.

We were circling over Spain. I stared out of the window as if I would see Andalusia, green lands and bullrings. As I focused on the abyss beneath the wings of the plane, the earth looked red under the glare of the sun, the buildings the size of pinheads. Beside me, a man was reading a newspaper. I noticed the word 'morning' in French. I had learned French in primary and secondary school, but I hadn't spoken it in over ten years. The man smiled and asked me in French where I came from. Egypt, I said in English, my voice sounding strange in my ears. The English word was clear but it was not *Misr*, the Arabic word.

The man repeated, 'Egypt?' in surprise, as though Egypt were the other end of the earth. His features looked strange: he had reddish skin, a long pointed nose and thin tight lips, and large hands covered with dark spots. I was overcome by feelings of alienation as I heard the man say: Is it your first time in Paris?

Swallowing hard, I replied: Yes.

At that moment, I wished the plane would take me back home. My daughter's eyes, filled with tears, beckoned to me. On the window were droplets of water like rain. The clouds changed colour and became heavy, dark and frightening. Between the gaps in the cloud, the ground appeared even stranger and further away. The man beside me abandoned his newspaper and closed his eyes, an air hostess was laughing with one of the passengers; a woman was reading a magazine and next to her a child played with small coloured blocks. Everything in the plane was safe and cosy.

The air hostess passed along with jugs of tea and coffee; the aroma of coffee was strong and my normal sensations returned, together with the sudden realisation that I was on the way to Paris.

Paris. The word is magic. None of the men in my family had ever visited Paris – in my childhood I had read of Egyptian men who had travelled there but the only two I remember now are Saad Zaghloul and Taha Hussein.

In my fantasy about Paris, beautiful blonde women dance on the banks of the Seine, their eyes blue, their legs smooth and pink, and the sound of music fills the universe.

The airport was huge and had many passages. I tried to follow the signs to reach the exit. The ground was shiny clean and sparkling and the faces of the people were fresh and pink, their bodies slim and fast moving. The high stiletto heels of the women rang on the ground briskly; the men's heels, too, were purposeful and brisk. Elegant bodies surged before me in quick and orderly succession, like the waves of a graceful river.

The streets of Paris were broad, the trees very green, the houses trim, their balconies hung with flowers. On no balcony did I see clothes spread out on a washing line.

I went down the steps to the metro. It was very crowded and fast-moving, but no one bumped into anyone else. In the seat facing me in the train, a girl and boy embraced each other, engrossed in a long kiss – although the train was packed, nobody looked at them. I tried to take my eyes off them. When the train stopped at the Champs Elysees, I rushed out and climbed the stairs to the street. Before me, I saw the great Arc de Triomphe and the wide street bordered by shops with huge glass windows. The faces around me looked radiant, their footsteps lively, their clothes chic, of various colours and styles, trousers glove-tight, dresses short.

Freedom was embodied before me; and it was contagious. I straightened my back, raised my head and strode with firm strides, swinging my arms. I bought a huge red apple, took a bite out of it and, with a group of young people, headed for a pleasure boat on the River Seine. Along both banks were buildings with wonderful domes and stone figures on top, like deities of old before a heavenly god appeared. The Eiffel Tower was an iron giant that sent a tremor through my body. A cold wind brushed my face and my heart was heavy, my chest filled with terror. I was unfamiliar with the sky above the towering walls of this city and this unfamiliarity stripped away pleasure and beauty.

In the Louvre, I wanted to throw my arms around him, his familiar features and huge head, his wide solid shoulders. As my fingers explored his shiny bronze body, the smell of the desert and the pyramids came back to me. Foreign tourists gazed at him with inquisitive blue eyes. The word 'Sphinx' sounded strange; for me, his name is *Abu al-Houl.* His resting place in the Giza Desert was more beautiful than his place here in the Louvre Museum. His eyes picked me out from among all the strange eyes – like me, he felt foreign and longed to return. I drew nearer and put my arms around him as if to lift him and return.

I spent a day wandering around the Louvre, passing among the various statues and paintings, then returning to *Abu al-Houl.* Beside him I felt soothed.

In one of the halls, I saw people gathered around Venus where she stood in all her splendour; goddess of beauty as they call her. She had one arm. I stared at her face to discover the secret of her beauty. Her features were quite ordinary. Beside her stood Athena, goddess of wisdom. People didn't look at her, even though she was more graceful than Venus, and more beautiful. Is wisdom in a woman undesirable and therefore un-attractive?

At the picture of the Gioconda or the Mona Lisa, I stopped for a while. It was the only painting behind glass. As the light reflected off it, I saw my own image inside the frame and not that of Gioconda. I moved my head to the left and to the right, but to no avail. Rows of people stood before the Gioconda in awe, each waiting their turn to see her close up. But as soon as they approached, the light reflected from the glass and they saw their own faces and not that of the Mona Lisa. Yet they turned away to leave their place to others, whispering: Wonderful! Wonderful!

An hour passed as I stood and gazed at the Gioconda, and saw my mother's face. Rationally, I knew that she was dead and buried in the overcrowded graveyard near *Jabal al-Muqattam* and that the face in front of me was that of the Mona Lisa, but all distinction between past and present had disappeared and scenes of my life from childhood unfolded one by one before my eyes. When I was a child, I had loved my father more than my mother. He was out of the house for half the day, did not scold me as my mother did when I went out without permission, and paid my school fees. But as I got older, I grew to love my mother more than my father. She would not go to sleep before I came home, prepared supper for me and sat with me so that I ate. At night, I would sense her walking in on tiptoe to cover me up.

I stared at the faces of the people standing in homage before the Gioconda. What dazzled them in da Vinci's lines? What moved deep inside them? Was it deep-down pleasure in the forbidden? Or was it the hidden hatred of the holy?

From the corner of my eye, I delved into people. No one looked at me, they were all held in the sway of art, or so it seemed to me. Even a priest standing in homage in his holy attire, even his eyes were filled with the magic of the Gioconda and her sinful attraction.

I walked along the banks of the Seine exposing my hot face to the cool refreshing wind. The sun was setting and the wooden kiosks displayed paintings and old books, reminding me of *al-Izbekiah*. Fruit was carefully laid out on shelves, flowers were multicoloured, people sat in cafés, in front of them gleaming trays, glasses and cups sparkling in the sunlight.

I noticed the domes of Nôtre Dame Cathedral, its ancient engravings and the sculptures standing under the light. In front of the huge door, a man sold dried, sweet-smelling plants in cloth bags and beside him, a man was selling coloured balloons. Tourists from different countries filled the place; some sat on the ground, eating and drinking beer from iced cans.

The wide vestibule inside the church was damp and dark. The candlelight created a mysterious and unearthly atmosphere with a smell of smoke or burning candles. When I was a child, damp and dark were associated with holy places, veined hands, lined faces, black robes, weak, wrinkled eyes swimming with

23

sadness. The majority were poor women. Why do women and the poor fear divine punishment more than others?

I looked up at the altar. A man and a woman were on their knees before the holy deity. Both displayed humility, but the woman's was greater. Her head was bowed, both eyes closed, but the man had one eye open and glanced at me, standing to the side.

Candlelight filled the hall with ghosts – a strange smell, like death. An old man with a long white beard muttered, a book in his hand, his eyes small and sunken beneath a pair of glasses, his drooping eyelids opening and closing with a fast regular movement, like those of my uncle Sheikh Abd al-Hamid. He was the youngest of my grandmother Mabrouka's thirteen stepbrothers from her father's four wives, and used to sit in the courtyard, a *Quran* on his lap, murmuring faintly. His drooping eyelids opened and closed rapidly with the movement of his head, yellow prayer beads between his fingers. The patter of his three wives' sandals never stopped, their high-pitched voices squabbling until sunset when each would go to bed in her own room. He would go to his first wife's room on Saturday night, rest for one night, then enter the room of his second wife on Monday night. The third wife was the youngest and was graced by Tuesday and Wednesday nights. On Thursday nights he rested.

His first wife once whispered in my ear: Your uncle will go to hell. He doesn't share out his nights fairly.

I did not understand what she meant. I was still a child and only knew that the week had seven nights. My uncle gave his wives four nights and rested on two. So where was the seventh night?

I asked him one day as he was sitting in the courtyard reading the *Quran*.

Friday night, he said, I give to Allah, for it is a blessed night.

In my small room on Saint Germain I lay on the bed, closed my eyes then opened them. I moved my head and saw the suitcase on the table. Hanging from its handle was a small red and white label with Paris written on it. I remembered with surprise where I was. It seemed strange to me, almost impossible. The room was not very different from any other room; a wardrobe, bed, closed window. My eyes remained fixed on the case, with its red and white label, to confirm that I really had come to Paris.

I got dressed and went out into the street. I sat on the pavement of a café facing the Luxembourg Gardens and the whole world passed before my eyes like a gushing river: faces from all four corners of the earth, all languages and accents. I stretched out my legs relaxedly, slowly sipping my coffee. Since that first visit to Paris, I love sitting in pavement cafés. On other visits, that seat in that café remained my favourite place. The Latin Quarter is the most beautiful area. My room in that small, elegant hotel on Boulevard St Germain, the bookshops and theatres and small cinemas where I sat on a warm, comfortable seat, stretched out my legs, and followed the scenes of authors from Shakespeare and Ibsen and Bernard Shaw and Chekhov to Molière and Sartre and Jean Genet.

I was still sitting in the café at three o'clock – I had two hours left before going to the airport to leave Paris. I ordered a large glass of beer and some long thin chips. The smell of the beer and its icy touch inside me was refreshing. I let my body sink further into the seat, closed my eyes, felt the warm rays of the sun on my eyelids. I never enjoyed sitting in cafés at home. Cafés in our country are for men. They sit on chairs, ogling the women passing by, from the front and from the back, from head to chest, then turn to examine the back of her legs and backside.

The sun vanished behind a grey cloud and the wind blew cold. I still had an hour left. I could walk to the metro station. I had a small suitcase which I towed along behind me on wheels. I don't take many clothes with me on journeys. I wash my clothes by hand, hang them up in the bathroom and find them dry in the morning.

I walked alongside the railings of the Luxembourg Gardens and decided not to go down into the metro station. I wanted to go on walking. I could walk to Albert Mayo Place and take a bus from there to the airport. Walking in the streets of Paris was so pleasant. But was there enough time? I looked at my watch. It had stopped.

I asked a woman passing by what time it was. She was

walking quickly, some books and files sticking out of the leather bag over her shoulder. Tall and slim, she was wearing sneakers, black trousers and a white wool jacket. She stopped walking, glanced at her watch and said:

– It's a quarter to four.

– Thank you, I said.

She looked up at me and I saw the shining blue in her eyes. I watched her smile and look at me, then heard her say, before quickly continuing on her way: *vous êtes belle, madame*. Her voice rang in my ears: *you are beautiful, madame*.

Before her words had sunk in, she disappeared. I spun round but saw only her back as she briskly walked away, a straight back inside a white wool jacket, a slender body and light, rapid strides.

It remained with me in the bus to the airport. Her image came back to me, the blue of her eyes as she smiled, her straight back and sprightly footsteps.

In the plane I stood looking out over Paris from the rear window. The lights were like clusters of pearls on red squares. I looked at my face in the mirror hanging above the washbasin, as if a new face were looking at me. The features resembled mine, but they seemed new. The skin glowed browner than ever, the eyes were larger, the black pupils more glittering. I whispered to the mirror: you are beautiful, madame. I used to whisper it silently so that no one should hear. Besides, there was no one at home who saw me as beautiful. I did not know why, but standards of beauty did not apply to me. In my heart of hearts I had other standards which I knew *did* apply to me. It was an instinctive knowledge that arose from deep inside myself with no confirmation from the outside world. And yet it was an absolute and certain knowledge – certainty itself.

However, no one around me told me I was beautiful. Not my father, not my mother. And grandmother Amna would purse her lips in distress, telling me I had inherited my father's brown skin. Grandmother Mabrouka would stare at my front teeth and pull a face saying: you've inherited fangs from your mother.

At school, when the girls were angry with me, they would tell me I was as tall and thin as a telegraph pole.

My mother did not regard my tallness as shameful, but she thought my little sister more beautiful than me because she had inherited her own white skin and soft hair.

My hair was not coarse, but it was not soft either and it had natural waves. But my aunt thought it coarse and she'd take me with her to the hairdresser to get it straightened out with fire-heated metal tongs. I can still smell burning hair and choke on the singeing and the smoke. I would pull my head away from between the hairdresser's hands and the tongs would scorch my ear or the tip of my nose.

When my maternal aunt had differences with my paternal aunt, my maternal aunt would accuse me of having frizzy hair and dark skin like my father's ancestors, and my paternal aunt would say that I got my 'fangs' from my mother's ancestors. My maternal aunt bought me a box of powder with which to hide my brown skin and my paternal aunt advised me not to open my mouth when I laughed. Her only remedy for my height was that I should walk with a hunched back.

I straightened my back and neck until my head touched the low ceiling of the aeroplane. I washed my face with *Eau de Cologne* to open up the pores of the skin and clear it of traces of powder.

My face always looks more beautiful in aeroplane mirrors than it does in the mirror at home or in any other mirror in the country. I don't know: do my features change simply by crossing borders, or are aeroplane mirrors of better quality?

PART TWO

The Other Half of the Earth

I inherited from my father his hatred of the ruler of Egypt and the English, and I was attracted only to men like my father. In medical school my first love was for a man who had decided to drive the English out of Egypt. But he did not drive out the English; instead the government drove him out and he died in prison.

In my mind, prison became associated with love. Whenever I heard of a man who was, or had been in prison, I felt my heart beating beneath my ribs. We met in the spring of 1964. Him and me alone. I asked him where he came from and he said, from prison. We laughed and filled our lungs with the air of *al-Muqqatam* hills and specks of dust. We got married but I bought no new clothes, only a dress for my daughter to wear on the day. We returned home carrying a large cake.

In the silence of the night, I put my head on his chest and my alienation ended. But in the street where we walked arm-in-arm, eyes stared at us with hatred. Signs of love between people are hated. On a moonlit night, we stopped the car beside the Nile and sat watching the light of the moon, our arms around each other. Suddenly a policeman pounced on the car. We told him we were married but he did not believe us. Signs of love between married people were unknown. Couples were supposed to live in a sea of hatred. The policeman would not be convinced until he saw the marriage certificate with its authorised signature and witnesses.

My husband was silent after thirteen years in prison. His skin was tanned by the sun of oases in the western desert, his face was thin and his eyes, raised in natural pride, were black and wide open to the sadness of the world. Whilst men around him chattered, he was silent. Droplets of spit from their revolutionary talk would spray the air as they waved their clenched fists and thumped them down on the table, whilst he was silent. They'd look at him uneasily out of the corners of their eyes – his silence pained them like a pinprick. His presence made them uncomfortable, for it revealed their falseness.

They tried to get rid of him, but he was the sort of person who remained in existence despite everything, like natural phenomena.

And I love nature and its phenomena. There is hostility between myself and things manufactured. I grew up amongst vegetation and crops growing under the sun and water flowing in the river, and I'd look at the birds in the sky and wish I could grow natural wings.

The wings before my eyes were manufactured from steel and not natural. Flying in the sky, my heart was heavy, travel no longer had its former appeal. I had left a daughter and husband at home. But I took with me a child as yet unborn. Beneath the seat belt, I felt it move, the small hand striking against the wall of my stomach, I wrapped the wool cover around me to keep it warm.

Beneath me, the vast yellow desert was divided by the River Nile, the two narrow banks branching out like black bands, the land between them shaped like a black triangle.

I rested my head against the back of the seat and closed my eyes. Two faces appeared through the window, signalling to me from a distant balcony, then dissolved into the air as though an invisible magical hand had snatched them away. The clouds were hazy and I was between the sky and the earth inside a closed metal box, heading for an unknown world.

My hands and feet were icy cold, like someone who has thrown herself into the ocean without knowing how to swim. But as the stewardess passed by with tea and coffee, the aroma of tea refreshed me and warmth spread through me; my imagination began to awaken like a sleeping giant – North America seemed to me like a new adventure, like virgin land which no one before me had discovered, not even Christopher Columbus.

*

My wristwatch pointed to ten o'clock exactly and the sun glowed on the horizon, whilst beneath it the curved white carpet of cloud looked like mounds of teased white cotton. The plane had crossed the desert and we were now over the sea. I closed my eyes and slept.

Yesterday I had slept fitfully, waking suddenly to look at the clock, imagining that the plane had taken off without me. Beside me my husband was sound asleep. I studied his features when his eyes were closed. His breathing was quiet, no snoring, no black moustache on his lip. He had opened his eyes and smiled:

– It's still early.

– I'm afraid I'll miss the plane, I said.

He wrapped his arms around me.

– If you miss it, nothing will happen. There are other planes.

But I imagined that if I missed this plane, there would not be another. My daughter was in the next room. She opened her eyes and smiled, then went back to sleep.

The ocean was still beneath the clouds and my watch pointed to 8.00: the sun had been set for over an hour in my homeland and night must have fallen.

But *I* saw the sun in the middle of the sky. A voice announced we would be landing at New York Airport in a few minutes and that it was one o'clock in the afternoon.

I moved the hands of my watch forward seven hours.

With every new journey, my imagination was fired, the desire to know kindled. But when I stepped onto new land, the fire went out and the delight vanished. Was I expecting a different kind of land? A different kind of people?

My feet struck the ground and I tested its firmness with the heel of my shoe. Under my feet its feel was like the other half of the globe, the hot humid air like the air of Egypt in summer.

New York Airport was huge, like Paris airport but larger. A black woman with large buttocks was wearing a hat with a red feather on it and shiny red shoes which clattered on the ground with small steps. Beside her was a tall skinny white girl, without buttocks, wearing tight green pants and rubber shoes,

yellow hair flying as she ran. A white man sitting on a seat
drank from a can of Coca Cola. Two short fat men with
Japanese features were running, each holding a black leather
case. A Chinese man scratched his head, his trousers flared
and so long they touched the ground. I ran with everyone
else to door of the helicopter. Its blades turned quickly and
it lifted off into the air without the door closing. Between
the towering New York skyscrapers were a number of lakes
and rivers. The helicopter moved between the tops of the
buildings and with every shake I grasped the seat in front of
me. The other passengers sat in their seats reading newspapers as though they were in a bus.

A few minutes later the helicopter landed and people poured
out of the door. I rushed with them towards the plane heading
south to Carolina.

Four hours' flying, then I heard the air hostess announce that
we were landing in Raleigh. The air was still and hot, hotter
than Cairo in August. And very humid. I felt the sweat under
my clothes and my hair stuck to my head. My palms were wet
and the suitcase slipped in my hand. I rushed for the nearest
taxi and asked for the university campus. The driver was white
and spoke English with a strange accent I didn't understand.
He pronounced only half the words and swallowed the other
half. He didn't open his mouth when he spoke, and it was as
though the words came out of his nose.

– What country are you from? he asked me.
– From Egypt.
– What do you do?
– I'm a doctor.
– Aha! Are there doctors in Egypt?
– Of course, like doctors in your country.
– Doctors here are very rich. You must be rich too, he said.

I saw him examine me in the front mirror. I imagined he
might take me off somewhere and rob me of all I had with me;
one case and thirty dollars.

– I am a doctor, but I'm poor, I said.
– This whole town's owned by four people – millionaires. We
live in the poor houses, me, my wife and four kids, said the
cab driver.

– Doesn't your wife work? I asked.

– What work? he said. And who'd look after the kids? I got a son sick with tuberculosis in a clinic on the other side of Raleigh.

I thought about the chest hospital and the queue of sick people. I pulled the window down. There was no air and my chest was choking with the humidity. Beside me was my case of clothes, a green ticket hanging from it on which were English letters that read 'Raleigh'. What was Raleigh? Was I really in America? What wonders of the world could I describe to my family when I returned home?

My room on campus was extremely hot and time passed slowly. I went down to the ground floor where the television was: Johnston was talking of peace and Vietnam. An American woman student sitting next to me spat at the screen and shouted: Liar!

Johnston's picture disappeared suddenly before he had finished talking and a half-naked woman danced on the screen, winking and drinking from a bottle called 'Wink'. She danced and licked her lips, kissed the mouth of the bottle and sang: Drink Wink. The woman vanished, Johnston reappeared and finished talking about peace.

The woman student stuck her feet in Johnston's face shouting: you talk of peace, then you send your soldiers with weapons to Vietnam!

She looked at me and asked where I came from.

Her name was Mary. She wore brief white shorts and blue sports shoes, tall and slender, with fair, shoulder-length hair. Her green eyes sparkled.

At the weekend she took me to her family in Chapel Hill, fifty miles from Raleigh. She drove her long large car along winding roads through a dense green forest of tall trees, houses dotted amongst the greenery. We pulled up in front of a small white house surrounded by a large garden. Her mother was planting flowers, her father was on a ladder painting windows. She put on a swimsuit and took me to the club swimming pool. She even drove the car wearing the swimsuit.

The toilet in the club had two doors. On one was written, for whites, on the other, for coloureds. I stood in front of the mirror to check the colour of my skin – I did not know which of the doors to enter. I went through the 'coloureds' door.

Mary returned to me without having swum and said angrily: Imagine! The swimming pool's closed for cleaning because two blacks went into it yesterday. This is a racist state! And she spat on the ground.

At night, she and her friend David invited me to go dancing. The small hall was crowded with young people, smoke, the smell of beer and dance music. All the heads had long hair, all the bodies wore tight trousers and the movements were free. I could hardly distinguish boys from girls. David asked me to dance, but I preferred to sit and drink beer while he danced with Mary, my eyes following their dance movements. With the beer in my veins, the dancing was contagious and I found myself moving my arms and head as I sat; then I got up and danced with them. Other young people joined us and began singing together and stamping on the ground in time to the music.

Since childhood I have loved dancing with strong movements. Eyes would stare at me in disapproval. A girl's muscles ought to be weak, her dance movements delicate and gentle. But girls' dancing never moved me; slow movements, slack muscles, the quiver of fat over the stomach and thighs, languid tunes full of wailing and weeping.

I left the dance floor and sat down, suddenly feeling sad. Mary came over and sat beside me. Surprised, she asked me:

– What happened?

– Young people in our country, I said, particularly the girls, don't have such freedom.

Her lips tightened, then she said:

– And we too don't have freedom. I love David but my father and mother don't like him because he's black.

– What will you do? I asked.

– We'll get married and leave the country. I want my children to live in a freer society.

The head of administration at the university was an elderly woman. Her eyes were blue and deep-set beneath her glasses which hung off a golden chain from her ears. Her glance under the lenses was piercing and felt like a burn on my face. She examined the brown colour of my skin as though measuring the degree of its brownness.

– The colour of my skin and the measurements of my body are a personal matter, I said to her.

Her mouth fell open, her glasses trembled and dropped onto her nose.

She grasped them in her hand and exclaimed: What did you say?

I let her continue staring at me, then gave her the form to see and said:

– Look, here are the entries for name, name of father, grandfather, address, sex, date of birth, marital status, religion, colour of skin and eyes, height, education certificates, character reference, lack of previous convictions or political crimes or imprisonment at any time, the number of awards received, physical disabilities.

The form was filled out. At each entry I had written the required information, carefully and exactly. At the box for previous convictions and crimes, I had written nothing for I had not yet been in prison. For religion, I wrote that of my father. For colour of eyes, I wrote *blackish*, then added the word *sparkling* in order to be precise. Also in order to be precise, in the entry for physical disabilities I wrote: *Black beauty spot on the back of neck.*

Despite all that, the university administrator continued to scrutinise me from head to toe, then said in a choking voice:

– But you did not put on the form that you were pregnant.

I searched for the box relating to pregnancy but did not find it.

– But there's nothing on the form . . . I said to her.

She interrupted me: Should a reputable university specify something like that on its forms?

– Something like that? I said angrily. What do you mean, something like that? Is pregnancy a sin?

I quickly took out of my bag my marriage certificate, with its signature of authoriser and witnesses. Her deep-set blue eyes widened in astonishment as she stared at the Arabic letters which must have looked to her like hieroglyphics or Chinese, the signature of the authoriser like a scribble.

– What language is this? she asked.

– It's Arabic, I said.

– Are you Egyptian or Arab? she exclaimed suspiciously.

– The Egyptians have been Arabs since the Arab conquest of Egypt in 640 AD by Omru bin al-'Aas.

I found myself and my baggage in a large bus heading north. The houses and streets of Raleigh receded, the state of North Carolina and its university were behind me. I opened the window and filled my chest with the refreshing air of the northern states. I felt like a released prisoner or a suffocated person emerging to the surface from underground.

Last night I had decided to travel to New York. How could I come to America and experience only a racist state in the south?

But in the morning I had heard from one of the Arab students that there was to be an important conference at Illinois University. So I found myself in a bus heading for Chicago.

I stood with seven hundred students singing in unison in Arabic:

We the young, ours is the morrow
and its eternal splendour
Our motto for all time
Long live the homeland, long live the homeland
For the day of sorrow we sold
our souls for no price

On the podium sat representatives of Arab countries, the governor of the state of Illinois, the dean of the university and representatives of American and Arab student unions. The president of the Arab Students Organisation was an Egyptian student named Ossama al-Baz. Amongst the other Arab personalities at the conference were Saadat Hassan and Dr Mohammed al-Mahdi who spoke on the role of oil in the Arab cause, Dr Burhan Hammad who talked about the Arab Gulf and Dr Rashad Murad, head of the permanent Arab League delegation to the United Nations in New York.

Amongst the Americans concerned with issues of the Arab countries was Harold Minor, head of the Middle East Friendship Society in America. He had worked as American Consul in Jerusalem for thirty years. In 1953 he had become the American Ambassador to Beirut, but then resigned from his post and devoted himself to the Arab cause in American universities.

Harold Minor was the first American I had ever heard speaking out against Zionism and against Johnson's policies. His words sounded strange to my ears, for I was not yet used to such expressions of opposition to the highest authority in the state. In our country, I had never heard anyone speak out against the existing regime.

I stretched out my legs in relaxation as I sat in my seat, feelings of freedom running warm through me like the movement of blood. Could there be, in our country, something called opposition?

A tall, thin American boy called Jack Sharir got up onto the platform, representing the American Students Union. He took the microphone and declared in literary Arabic that the American Students Union had taken a resolution supporting the return of the Palestinians to their homeland and compensation for all their losses. He attacked Johnson's policies in the Middle East and in Vietnam, describing them as immoral.

When he got down from the platform, my eyes followed him until he returned to his seat, imagining that policemen would surround him and haul him off to prison.

The American student sitting beside me heard me say: Nobody has taken him to prison.

– You only go to prison here if you are a threat to the system, he said. Such speeches and conferences are no threat.

– Do you have political prisoners here? I asked.

– Many, he said.

My relaxation dissolved and the muscles of my body tensed again. I left the hall and went into another, on the walls of which hung the paintings of Palestinian artists Aissa Abd al-Majid and Ismail Shamout. The tragedy of the Palestinian people was embodied in their lines: a mother stood in the open before a black tent, clasping a child to her chest. A young man carried arms, his eyes turned towards the plundered homeland.

*

Six days of conference ended with resolutions and the election of seven new members to the executive council of the Arab Students Organisation and a new president. At the end of the conference a sheet of paper with the resolutions was passed to us. I put it in my bag.

As I was leaving, I saw a queue of elderly American men entering the same hall. They were wearing military clothes, like the uniforms soldiers wore in the nineteenth century, on their heads black caps decorated with white ostrich feathers. I found out they were on their way to conference number 109 for old soldiers in the state of Illinois.

In my seat on the bus making for the East Coast of America, I opened my bag and began reading the paper which had been given us:

> The 14th Conference of the Arab Students Organisation
> in America has passed a number of resolutions concerning
> various Arab issues, recommending financial and moral
> support for the Palestine Liberation Organisation to
> help build a Palestine liberation army; supporting the
> resolutions of the Arab summit conferences; backing
> the Jedda Accord and proposing a united plan for using
> Arab oil in the service of the Arab cause. The conference
> declares its support for the armed revolutionary struggle
> to liberate the occupied south and calls for the
> establishment of a united front of progressive Arab
> forces to confront imperialist plans and to liberate the
> Arab Gulf and Oman and to develop this region
> economically, culturally and socially through the Arab
> Development Fund. It calls on the government of
> Kuwait to prevent non-Arab infiltration into this
> region. The conference appeals to progressive Arab
> movements and governments to assist the Arabistan
> Liberation Front and support the government of Sudan
> in finding a solution to the problem of the south to
> safeguard the unity of Sudan and thwart the divisive
> imperialist conspiracy against it. The conference also
> recommends increasing the publicity campaign of the

Arab students in America and Canada, particularly in regard to the development of American policy towards the Middle East.

I still have this sheet of paper in my bag. Although twenty years have passed since these resolutions were made, it seems as though they were taken yesterday.

In New York, I met the Dean of Columbia University. I gave him a form, complete with details, to which I had added a new box concerning pregnancy, in front of which I wrote: *Four months' pregnant.*

The dean smiled and said:

– All these are personal matters. The university does not require this information.

– But the University of South Carolina . . . I said.

– Don't think that all universities in America have such a backward mentality, he said.

I lived in Manhattan, in the heart of New York. My favourite place is always at the heart of things, feeling the throbbing pulse of life. Here, everything moved with vitality. In Greenwich Village people sat in pavement cafés as in Paris, eating and drinking and talking. Young people sat on the grass in Washington Square near New York University. A group of young people played guitars and sang and danced as people gathered round.

One day, Marion took me to a large meeting at which Dr Stoughton Lind, an American professor at Bell University, was talking. His passport had been taken away from him because he had been to Vietnam on a fact-finding trip and returned to organise demonstrations against the war in Vietnam.

Marion introduced me to him, saying: this is a colleague of mine at Columbia University. She's an Egyptian doctor.

I recall Stoughton Lind saying to me that day that the problem of Palestine was no less serious than the problem of Vietnam, but that Zionist forces in America owned the banks and the media.

– Why don't you go on a fact-finding trip to the Middle East like you went to Vietnam? I said to him.

He laughed and said: When I get my passport back from the government.

The edge of the letter in the mailbox showed through the glass: the most beautiful sight in America, more beautiful than the Statue of Liberty in the middle of the ocean, better than Fifth Avenue and its skyscrapers, better than the famous Rockefeller Park in the centre of New York with its multicoloured fountains and flowers and people from all over the world, better than the wonderful music and dancing on the ice-rink. The postage stamp on the letter had a picture of the pyramids on it and the word 'Egypt'. On the envelope was my name in large round letters, the movement of slender fingers around a pen in our shared study in the small flat at the top of Pyramid Street.

In the long letter, my husband said he had bought a new lamp for the study and had read some books he hadn't read before, that our daughter was well, was going to school every morning and that before she went to sleep he told her a beautiful story.

I put the letter under my pillow. At night I re-read it. In the morning, I put it in my bag with my papers and books, and at lunch, I chewed my food slowly and read it again.

At night, by lamplight, I sat in bed under the covers and read it. On the wall above my desk hung a wall calendar for 1965. Before going to bed, I crossed out the day that had just ended and counted the days that were left.

Then I turned out the light and lay back on the pillow. I could hear the pounding of my heart and feel a gentle movement against the walls of my stomach, like delicate arms of velvet. I wondered when he would see the light of day.

In Sloane Hospital next to Columbia University, I went to see Dr Todd.

He examined me, then said: I expect the birth to be within a week.

We were at the beginning of December, the white snow was glistening on the windows and streets. He smiled and said:

– You're lucky! The birth will come with the Christmas holiday and the New Year.

Marion agreed to go with me to Broadway to buy clothes for the child. My American women colleagues in the university exclaimed: we don't buy clothes for the child until after the birth. Wondering why, I discovered that some superstitions are still alive and well in America. Buying clothes before the birth of a child is a bad omen that may mean it will die before or during birth. But I had seen my mother buying baby clothes before a birth and she had given birth to three boys and six girls without one of them dying. Neither had my grandmother believed in such a superstition.

– These American women are still backward, Marion said to me.

– And you? Aren't you American, Marion? I asked her.

– Yes, she replied, but I've freed myself from such nonsense, the first being hatred of black skin.

– And second? I asked.

– Whitening my face with make-up, she said.

Simple and natural and full of life, she was as excited by scientific lectures as by political demonstrations. Her skin was clear and without make-up, her hair free and left to the wind and rain. We walked together in the street like children.

I did not feel strange with her, but as though we'd been born in the same country and had spent our childhood to–gether. A vast distance separated me from other American women.

Saturday 9 December 1965. I recall that night despite the passing of the years. Marion invited me to go to the Guggenheim Museum in the morning and I invited her to see the play *A View from the Bridge* by Arthur Miller in the afternoon.

We walked to the corner of 88th Street and Fifth Avenue where the Guggenheim Museum was. It had opened in 1959, designed by the architect Frank Wright in an organic fashion; a new kind of building that studies a place in relation to human beings and looks at how space can be used to appear larger and more pleasing to the eye.

Everything had rounded lines, the walls, the stairs, the storeys. Circles appeared longer, with no beginning or end, and gave the illusion of movement, like a living thing. The place was turned into something resembling an organic body and was imbued with a vague sort of warmth and comfort.

We went from floor to floor. Three thousand paintings of modern art of the nineteenth and twentieth centuries.

On one of the paintings were engraved Jackson Pollock's words: *Painting is struggle*.

I was aroused by Marion's voice saying: Do you understand anything of these lines?

– I don't think so, I said, but I'm trying.

A moment of silence passed, then I asked her: What is the substance of struggle?

– What struggle? said Marion.

– The substance of modern art, I said. It's a new philosophy, not new materials or tools.

– What's the new philosophy in these senseless lines without shape or meaning? I don't understand any of this nonsense!

We were silent a moment, studying the lines. Then Marion said:

– Anyway, art is felt, not understood.

– Are feelings and understanding separate? I wondered.

– What do you mean? she said.

– Feelings are understanding. I feel therefore I understand.

– I understand therefore I feel, she laughed.

– What do you feel? I asked her.

– Hungry!

We laughed and left the Guggenheim Museum for a small restaurant where we ate grilled meat. After lunch, we went on to Broadway where *A View from the Bridge* by Arthur Miller was showing.

The theatre was crowded and we could only get back seats. I had to crane forward to hear the actors but I only caught halves of sentences as they were delivered in a rapid American accent. The audience laughed at jokes I could not hear. When I saw Marion laughing with the audience I asked her if she had heard the joke?

– No, she said, but laughter's contagious. And we laughed.

We left the theatre before the end and walked along Fifth Avenue, the biggest street in New York. The coolness was refreshing. The huge windows of the stores sparkled with lights and candles in preparation for the Christmas holidays and the New Year. Behind the glass were coloured fountains, mannequins moving and dancing under the lights, new displays of fur coats, hats, jewellery, electrical appliances of every type and kind that turned in the revolving windows. And a crowd of people from all countries of the world.

In front of one of the huge glass windows was a large group of people jostling for a view. Children climbed onto their mothers' and fathers' shoulders to see what was there.

– Maybe there's a magician behind the glass! I said to Marion.

We made our way forward. Under the coloured lights we saw what appeared to be a large electric oven and inside it an egg as large as a duck's. The egg moved on its own, then it broke and a live chick with spindly legs came out of it.

The children laughed and clapped their hands, young men and women kissed and danced, adults gawped in surprise and a man whispered to his wife: this is a time of miracles. Everything is made by machines, even chicks!

– Soon we'll be making babies in test-tubes and women will be freed from pregnancy and birth, Marion said and everyone laughed.

On the way home, I felt a bit dizzy. Marion was driving and when she saw I was quiet, she asked: Are you tired?

– No, I said.

– It's been an exhausting day, but it was great, she said.

At my door she wished me good night, then drove off to her house.

It was eleven-thirty when I got undressed and put on my nightdress. Suddenly I felt pains. Was it labour? I was completely alone. Confused, I sat on the edge of the bed. The pain subsided for a while but soon returned. I realised it *was* a labour pain. The telephone was on the bedside table. Should I call Marion? But we had had a long and tiring day and she needed to sleep. It was midnight and I could not call anyone at such a time of night, not even my mother.

Sloane Hospital was ten minutes' walk from my place. I put on my thick wool coat, stuffed the new baby clothes into a bag and went out into the street. The air was frosty. It was pitch black and the street was deserted. I walked quickly, then began running. My fingers and toes were frozen and I shivered with both cold and fear. A long black shadow was following me, the heels of his shoes rapping on the ground. I stopped for a moment and turned round. There was nobody there. It was only my own shadow on the ground and the sound of my own feet on the paving stones. The sound stopped for a moment as a sharp pain in my back brought me to a standstill, and my body slumped and doubled up. Should I sit down on the pavement? If I sat, would I give birth in the road?

The lights of the hospital blinked at me from afar, further than they really were. I would never reach it. I tensed my back muscles and said to myself: I'll get there, I won't stop until I reach the hospital. I don't know how my feet began to walk again or how I covered the remaining distance with such strong, regular and uninterrupted strides, but a sudden and strange kind of willpower grew like a new limb from my body as though a new body had replaced the old one. New legs carried my body quickly and lightly and, beside me, I saw the shadow of my body accompanying me with the same movement. The activity dispelled the awful silence and kept me company in the darkness like a comrade.

As soon as I arrived at the hospital that extraordinary energy and that new body vanished and I felt my old body reappear suddenly, then collapse onto the nearest seat. I did not move after that except on a stretcher that a nurse pushed ahead with both hands to the delivery room. The smell of iodine and ether, the whiteness of the walls and the uniforms of the nurses filled me with a deep comfort and joy.

I saw Dr Todd's face before me. He smiled as he told me I would have a beautiful baby. He wanted to put a gas mask over my face, but I refused it for I wanted to give birth to my child fully conscious. I knew that they took babies away immediately after birth and put them in a glass room with dozens of other newly borns and a terrifying feeling came over me that my child would get mixed up with the others.

But the pains got stronger and so intense I thought I would die. I asked for gas. Before Dr Todd put the mask over my face, I said to him:

– Give me a mild drug so that you can wake me when the baby's born and let me see him before he's taken to the baby room.

Dr Todd smiled and said:

– I promise, but that depends on you too and on your ability to come round quickly from the drug.

The smell of ether filled my nose and mouth. A strange coldness ran through my body, moving quickly from my head to my chest, then to my legs and feet. I felt as though I was falling into a deep, dark and airless well and opened my mouth to shout for help, but to no avail. I had become a dead and motionless body, with a strange heaviness like the whole globe on my eyelids.

Suddenly, I saw my mother before me. She was wearing a silky yellow robe, a white transparent shawl around her neck. Her honey-brown eyes looked into mine as I lay on the bed. In surprise I said: how did you know, and how did you get here from a country so far away?

I used to hide all my pains from her, even labour pains. I did everything painful alone, without my mother, without my father. But my joys I did not experience alone; my mother or father had to be with me. I always used to surprise them with my joys. My mother felt my pains before I did and no matter how far away I was, she knew where I was and came. I was alone in the house that night in the spring of 1956 when I was pregnant with my daughter and suddenly felt labour pains: I did not know it was labour. Blood flowed copiously. The head of my daughter was large and did not want to come down. My muscles were firm and inflexible. I could have bled to death. Suddenly the doorbell rang and there was my mother. I don't know how she knew or how she came or who opened the door for her. All I knew was that I had been alone in the house, that my mother was in another house far away and that nobody but me knew I was bleeding.

The heaviness left my eyelids. I opened my eyes in astonishment. My mother's face looked strange. For the first time I saw her wearing glasses, her eyes blue and not honey-coloured. I said to myself: maybe her face has changed, because she's been dead for years. I heard a man's voice ringing in my ears in a foreign lanaguage.

– Look! It's a beautiful boy!

The fog lifted and I saw a strong white light and white walls, the snow-white coat of the doctor, his deep blue eyes under his glasses, his wide smile and shining teeth and his voice ringing in my eyes like pure silver.

– Look! It's a beautiful boy!

I stared at the small face in amazement. His skin was red with my blood, lots of black hair, delicate nose, the eyes closed and the mouth open and panting. Then he closed his mouth and opened his eyes. My eyes fixed on the black shining pupils; the image engraved itself on my mind and became part of me. I heard Dr Todd's voice say laughingly: Are you memorising his features?

The nurse lifted him up and he cried and kicked out with his arms and legs. Then she put him on a white table and tied a white nylon tag around his small wrist with the number 9578. Another nurse took my hand and tied a nylon bracelet around my own wrist with the same number.

I closed my eyes and slept with the memory of those black eyes in my mind and number 9578 on my wrist.

In the morning I opened my eyes to see a tray beside me, on it a pot of tea, boiled egg, butter and toast. I ate with relish, then jumped out of bed and walked along the long corridor until I reached the glass room. I pressed my face to the window, searching for a pair of black pupils amongst the similar newborns, and found them. My heart pounded and I raised my hand to wave at him through the window. But he was lying in his small white bed staring at the ceiling, his fingers in his mouth.

A nurse came running towards me saying in surprise: You gave birth at one in the morning and it's eight o'clock now. Only seven hours and you're walking like this along the corridor?

– Movement after giving birth is good, I said to her. Besides, my child is hungry and I must feed him now.

I returned to bed and presently saw the nurse wheeling a small glass bed towards me in which was my child. I picked him up and put him to my breast. I saw the small mouth panting when I put the dark nipple between his lips; his jaws grasped onto it and he began sucking the milk with relish, his five small fingers tightly wrapped around mine. A rush of maternal feelings flooded through me as warm as the flow of blood in my veins.

Three days later I asked to leave the hospital where I only saw my child at feeding times and he slept in a room far from me. I wanted to hold him in my arms, for us to be in the same room. Besides, the smell of the hospital had lost its pleasure and staying only meant more expense.

I gave them a cheque and they gave me my son's birth certificate. I found they had given him my father's name. I was surprised. Do they name a child here after the mother? The staff nurse, whose name was Mrs Silverman, asked in surprise: Don't you carry your husband's name?

– No, I said. I carry my father's name.

Mrs Silverman must have thought I was an unmarried mother since in American law a married woman carries her husband's name and only unmarried mothers keep their father's name, in which case the child takes the mother's name and is regarded as perfectly legitimate.

– I am married but I bear my father's name, I said. That's the law in Egypt.

– How strange! Mrs Silverman gasped in astonishment. Don't women take their husband's name in your country?

– No, I said.

– How strange, Mrs Silverman repeated. Then she thought for a moment and said: an Egyptian wife is luckier than an American woman because she has one name throughout her life. Here a woman changes her name after marriage and may change it more times if she marries more often.

She told me the strange story of her three names. Before marriage her name was Miss Silverman. She married a man named Brown and her name became Mrs Brown and she got her nursing certificate under this name. Then she got divorced from Brown and two years later married Morgan. After marrying him, she got her master's degree in nursing under the name of Mrs Morgan. She separated from her husband Morgan three years later and her name became Mrs Silverman, her father's name. The previous year she got her doctorate in nursing under the name Mrs Silverman.

At the end of her story she said sadly:

– So I've got three university certificates, each with a different name.

– What a test of a woman's personality, I said to myself.

But this was at the end of 1965 and America had not yet heard of the women's liberation movement. It did not occur to me then that only a few years later American women would take to the streets to demonstrate against male domination and against laws which make a woman inferior to a man, including the law which makes a wife take her husband's name.

Four days later I went back to college. The news spread through the university and teachers and colleagues came to my house to congratulate me, each of them bringing a present for the child. One of these was a small carriage with a pretty red hood. On warm days when the sun shone I went to the park on the banks of the Hudson river, pushing the carriage in front of me. Peeping out from under the red hood was the small face with two gleaming black pupils that widened in surprise at any sound or movement, the small lips open in a happy smile. His laughter sounded like the cheep of a bird. Women walking by stopped to look at the sparkling black eyes and exclaimed, Isn't he cute! What a beautiful baby!

His eyes, like mine, widened in surprise: women in our country do not stop or show their admiration of a child, no matter how beautiful he is, but will even say, how ugly he is! And the mother smiles with joy, assured of protection from the evil eye.

My son was a calm, quiet child and slept throughout the night and day, waking only to be fed. I would leave him asleep after the morning feed and go to college. From home to college was seven minutes' brisk walk and I'd run back at three o'clock to feed him.

On holidays Marion helped me clean the house, wash the baby's clothes and do the shopping. At weekends, I took colour photos of him to send to my husband and daughter. He became my comrade. During the day he kept me company with his chuckles, the movement of his hand when he shook the coloured balls fixed onto his chair, his small fingers when he grasped mine not wanting to let go.

In the darkness of the night filled with loneliness, with the whistle of the ocean wind, the beat of the rain against the skyscraper windows, the creak of the huge black posts on the metal bridges, in the darkness of the night in the heart of that vast American city thousands of miles from family and country, I opened my eyes in the dark as I lay under the covers shivering with the cold of alienation, my heart heavy with loneliness and desolation; raising my head from the pillow, I saw him sleeping in his little bed, his skin the colour of mine, his features like mine, in his warm breath the smell of family and country.

I took him in my arms and closed my eyes, feeling the warmth run through me. The wind stopped whistling, the night was no longer strange and desolate, and I slept until I heard him in the morning. The birds chirped and he waved his arms and legs in the air and tried to lift his head to look at me through the posts of his coloured bed.

He was growing quickly and ate with appetite. Baby food from a small glass jar, an instant and tasty kitchen. Jars of various shapes and colours filled the shelves of shops and supermarkets. Fruit, vegetables, meats, fish, eggs and food of all kinds. On the apple jar was a picture of a red apple, on the fish jar a coloured fish in the hand of a child, on the milk and rice jar a white bowl full of rice pudding.

How much time my mother could have saved, instead of standing in front of the stove mixing milk into the ground rice to make *mahalabiyya*! How much time I could have saved making my daughter's food when she was a child! Here, I reach out and take the baby food out of a jar.

I was getting used to my new life, growing to love college and lectures, and new friendships bound me to men and women colleagues. My professors were surprised to see me hand in papers on time. I got the highest marks in the exams and throughout the whole year only missed four days.

One of the research papers I presented was on Harlem Hospital in the black district of New York. I visited the hospital a number of times with Marion. The waiting hall reminded me of the one in *Qasr al-'Aini* hospital, the queues like the ones before me every morning; tired wan faces, sad lustreless eyes, waiting for the moment the nurse called them in to be seen by the doctors. Some were bleeding, some semi-conscious, crowded into the hall for long hours.

– Why do they wait so long? I wondered.

– Not enough doctors, Marion said. One doctor examines a hundred patients a day.

In my diary for 1956, when I was an intern in *Qasr al-'Aini*, I noted the number of patients I saw in the outpatients clinic in one day. On one of them, the number was one hundred and twenty-three. When I moved to the Ministry of Health, there was no longer any means of knowing how many were in the queues that stretched as far as the eye could see.

The wards in Harlem Hospital looked like the wards in *Qasr al-'Aini*. But in *Qasr al-'Aini* the passageways were clear. Here I saw patients lying on extra beds in the passageways and narrow hospital corridors. The smell was the same: the decay of blood and pus and festering wounds. From the lavatories came the putrid odour of overflowing drains, around which red and black cockroaches, big and small, ran.

Marion put a handkerchief to her nose saying:

– They throw surplus tins of food into the ocean whilst these people are sick from hunger.

– Why does this happen? I asked her. America's a rich country.

– Yes, said Marion. We have an obesity problem, the problem of the wealthy. Twenty-five per cent of Americans are overweight from eating too much. But a capitalist economy requires that there are poor people. They are the ones who buy from the market and if the surplus was distributed to them they would not go shopping. This would lower buying power, goods would accumulate, and company and factory owners would lose.

I learned something new each day. For my research, I chose sensitive and difficult subjects. The relationship between economy and medicine, health and illness. The reasons for poverty in America. Conditions for black people in Harlem and millionaires in Manhattan. The rate of tuberculosis in the Brooklyn district. The relationship between social justice and health. There were no restrictions in research. I chose the subjects I wanted. There was no security service in the university and no police guard. Professors not only taught but learned as well. Lectures were not just for students to listen and write in their notebooks, but were a dialogue between professors and students, an open dialogue and discussion. Professors admitted to mistakes and knew each student well. A kind of humanity and spirit of fellowship pervaded the university.

I awoke in the morning to cool, refreshing air which filled me with enthusiasm and energy as I went to college. My feet sped across the ground with light and easy steps as though I'd been born here, would die here, and knew no other place. The sound of wheels racing across the iron bridge grew familiar, and steam rising from holes in the ground. Trains running underground, helicopters flying like birds between the skyscrapers, the smell of the ocean, reading the morning papers, the shouts and clamour of demonstrations. The night rain washed the ground, the air and the buildings and everything gleamed in the sunlight.

Marion's blue eyes were gleaming too as she met me at the door: Demonstration today!

From childhood I have loved demonstrations, a secret passion for any demonstrator rebelling against the regime, longing and waiting for a disruption in the universe, any disruption, even a star falling from the sky or the earth quaking to the sound of thunder and lightning.

Marion handed out long yellow leaflets. One photo was of a child in Vietnam, her face burned with napalm. Another was of a one-armed American soldier lying on the ground, blood pouring from his head and a Vietnamese soldier trying to lift him. The street was full of young people, men and women, mothers pushing baby carriages, carrying banners and shouting: *We want peace not freedom*. A demonstration of older men and women carrying a large poster on which was written, *Bring our sons back from Vietnam!*

Columbus Square vibrated with the noise and shouts. The March sun hung in the sky with the first tidings of spring. Fervor ran through me like warm blood. The shouts had a familiar ring, like the shouts of students back home. The faces were like those of my family, white, black, brown, all of them alike, forming one human body. And I was part of this body, their breathing mine, their fervor mine, the final dissolution of the last drop of alienation and loneliness in my blood.

On the last day of the academic year, we were given our certificates at a big party. The dean presented me with a certificate written on burnished paper and another, unwritten certificate which rang through the air in his quiet voice, the words engraving themselves in my mind and becoming part of me, remaining as alive as brain cells.

The certificates written on paper have lain at the bottom of my desk for twenty years. The paper has yellowed and the letters have faded with time. But all the unwritten certificates have remained alive in my mind, live with me and will die with me. I still remember what the nature teacher said to me in primary school in 1942. I remember every single word and the movement of her lips as she said them, the movement of her eyes, her voice brushing my ear and running through the deep channels inside my head, flowing through the cells warmly like a surge of new blood.

There were tears in Marion's blue eyes. She waved to me from behind the window, then vanished. My eyes widened in surprise as a fine mist like rain drizzle covered the pane. A warm tear fell onto the back of my hand and my heart was heavy.

A voice came from the roof of the plane announcing it would take off for Cairo in a few minutes and the air over my head seemed to vibrate like an electric current. Two faces signalled to me from our small house at the beginning of Pyramid Street, the green tree overlooking the wall in front of the house, Uncle Ahmed the doorman sitting on the bench, the newspaper kiosk on the corner of the street, the *ful* seller pushing a long ladle into the mouth of a steaming pot, the junk dealer shoving a cart before him, his head thrown back, shouting: Any old iron!

Longing crept through my body. My eyes searched for familiar features, my ears listened for accents and voices. Suddenly I longed for everything and anything at home, even the specks of dust swimming in the air under the rays of the sun and the smell of sewers carried by the spring breeze in the early morning.

My eyes preceded the rapid wheels towards the ground and the pounding of my heart smothered all other sounds. I glued my face to the window to look at the hundreds of heads on the terrace of the airport. There were many strange faces and my eyes darted from one to another looking for particular features. The slender face and deep black eyes; the small round face with honey-coloured eyes.

Suddenly I saw the two of them, as if particles of air had thickened and gathered to materialise them before my eyes. My husband was waving to me with quiet, confident movements and my daughter was jumping up and down at his side. She rushed towards me, indifferent to the police cordon, but a policeman pushed her back.

I raised my hand as if to touch her, but she was still far away. My clothes and those of the baby were strewn on the wooden bench in front of the customs officer. His fingers toyed with my papers and books. I had nothing with me except children's toys and a blue aeroplane with delicate white wings for my daughter. The officer pulled the plane out of its cardboard box tied with a coloured ribbon. He shook it violently to make sure there was nothing inside it. It slipped from his hand and fell onto the floor and the delicate wings shattered on the asphalt like a white butterfly.

Joy and small sadnesses drowned in the embrace. I emerged from the airport with arms around me. My husband, my daughter, friends and relations. In my arms I carried my son, a new member of the small family.

PART THREE

The Jordan Valley and the Banks of the River

In June 1966, I returned to my homeland from America. In June 1967, the defeat happened. Defeat was in the air and I breathed it before it happened.

Flags and triumphal arches were put up over every inch of land, nationalist songs were broadcast over microphones day and night. But my mind and body sensed defeat in the bowing of the triumphal arches at the slightest breeze, in the inflection of the voices that grew hoarse, like a sob, at the end of each song, in the eyes under lowered eyelids on platforms.

On the fifth day of June I saw birds in the sky flutter in panic, then fly away as if it were a winter day with thunder and lightning warning of rain. It was the height of summer, no thunder, no lightning and no rain. But the skies changed suddenly, with the boom of planes faster than the speed of light; distant, muffled explosions; a few minutes later the skies returned to normal.

It was early morning and I did not know what had happened. I went to the TB hospital as usual. For the first time, there was no queue of patients lined up as far as the eye could see. But they were sitting in the hospital courtyard, ears pressed to a small radio, cheering and clapping. A nurse came over to me, shouting eagerly: So far, we've shot down fourteen enemy planes!

I never believed official broadcasts or newspapers or statements. But I did believe her. I was exhausted. Every day I inhaled the breath of tuberculosis patients without a protective mask. In the triangle under my ribs was a pain that accompanied me each morning like nausea, dissipating my sixth sense and weakening the other five so that I did not smell the stench

59

of sewage in the pool in front of the hospital nor hear the groaning of the queues. My skin, too, had lost its sense of touch.

I believed the nurse immediately. The chronic pain under my ribs vanished, my nausea lifted and with it the blackness. I shouted with joy: Then it's victory, not defeat! And rebuked myself for my black feelings and inability to foresee anything but disaster. But half a minute later I came to my senses. I saw the long queue return with wan faces, bowed heads, defeated eyes. The smile on the nurse's face froze and the blood drained from it as we learned that all our planes had been hit as they sat stationary on the ground. The nurse said apologetically: I wasn't lying to you, doctor, but I really believed the radio.

Defeat took the shape of reality, and reality took the shape of a long pale face, a long pale nose, and large pale eyes that held every defeat in the world.

The homeland became funereal. We awoke to the sound of a voice reciting the *Quran* and went to sleep with the same monotonous recitations. The dead had not yet been buried and still walked on the earth, looking at us each day with murdered eyes whilst the murderers' eyes shone with victory, as they marched on the soil of the homeland. The battlefront became three fronts and more.

A plane took me to the battlefront in Jordan. In my bag was medical and not war equipment, but in my head was a decision to train to shoot and fight. In the world around me it was either kill or be killed, and I did not want to be killed. I had done some weapons' training in 1956, after the tripartite (English–French–Israeli) attack on Port Said. At the time I had been a country doctor in my village of Tahla. The medical unit had been transformed into a camp for weapons' training and nursing. Men carried weapons and fought, women dressed wounds – division of labour on the basis of sex in war as well as peace. I said: I will carry arms and fight, not dress wounds!

I trained in shooting and target practice. The military trainer was surprised that a woman could hit a target first go. He gave me the masculine name 'captain' as a sort of distinction in marksmanship. But I refused the male name and kept my own.

– It's an honour for you to be given a man's name, he had exclaimed.

When I called him by a woman's name, he grew angry.

– It's an honour for you to be given a woman's name! I exclaimed.

He raised his rifle and aimed it at my head. I raised mine and aimed it at his. He immediately retreated, and since that moment I have realised that men only understand weapons and that weapons are only defeated by weapons. I hate the feel of a weapon in my hand and I hate the sight of blood, but I hate rape even more; the rape of women's rights or the rape of the homeland. Both of them are rape, both are the two faces of one evil deed – slavery or oppression by armed force.

In Amman Airport, I saw a number of young *fedayeen*. Their eyes had a spark that reflected the colours of the mountains and reminded me of the mountainous features I had seen in Algeria. Revolution makes features attractive.

Eyes at home were dull and full of defeat, and defeat robs the features of beauty. The movement of the body becomes slow, glances are averted and eye does not meet eye. Arms hang limply and the mind is listless. Since childhood I have hated defeated faces: the face of Aunt Na'amat after her husband divorced her, of Uncle Yahya after he failed his studies.

In command headquarters in Amman, I met the leaders, all of them men. Their eyes darted about constantly in all directions. They spoke ceaselessly and listened only to themselves. One of them wore the uniform of *al-Sa'iqa*, around his middle a wide, decorated belt from which hung weapons. His fingers were soft and his nails were polished and clean and had never touched the soil. His skin was white and untouched by the summer sun or the heat of the earth. His voice had a metallic ring that echoed like the voice of an invisible god and changed to loud orders without him moving his lips.

I feel suffocated when such wretched circumstances bring me to sit amongst the gods in command headquarters or presidential office or ministry, or wherever the leadership is. Leadership in our country was authority and authority privilege.

As I sat in command headquarters, my eyes met those of a

young *feda'i*; I realised from his eyes that he was a fighter and not a member of the leadership. His gaze was frank and direct, eye to eye. His hand, too, shook hands and his arm was straight. He had one arm only, for he had lost the other in Palestine. And one leg, the other one amputated above the knee after the Battle of Karameh on 21 March, 1968.

I was still staring at the face of the young *feda'i*. Later, he looked at the road ahead as he sat beside the driver, weapons in his one and only hand. The vehicle was an armoured jeep. I sat behind the driver, beside me three armed *fedayeen*, including a young woman named Asma; her eyes had the same spark and steady gaze as those of the boys. Behind me sat Um Youssef, a middle-aged woman with fine features like those of my aunt Bahiya, her head covered in a white shawl. They called her *Um al-Fedayeen* – mother of the guerrillas. The car brought us to al-Karameh, and desolation and destruction. The stagnant, heavy air of silence moved now and again to the sound of a muffled explosion. All the houses were destroyed, wires were cut, and the cars were like pieces of black charcoal. No inhabitants, nothing except stones and the scattered remains of houses and furniture, a child's shoe, the smell of dried blood and burned trees.

I walked with the *fedayeen* amongst the rubble. A tall, slim youth appeared from nowhere, a black and white *kuffiya* around his head; he led us to a nearby underground cave on the river bank and to a group of young people waiting in a state of armed readiness, their eyes fixed on the West Bank, longing to return to the land of their birth from which they had been driven out by force. The land beyond the Jordan river, the high green bank, looked down on them. Homeland and family wrenched apart between two river banks: a murdered mother lying under the walls; a father stabbed in the chest, stomach and back; a child of whom all that remained was a single shoe. From the homeland where Israel now was, mortars showered them with bombs and American-made aeroplanes fired rockets and napalm bombs.

At a signal from one of the young men, we all dived into the cave, the walls of which shook to the sound of mortar and artillery fire. Dust fell from the roof which was as black as the earth, coarse and cracked. Scratched on the walls in squiggly hand-writing was a poem of Mahmoud Darwish:

> *The lash of the executioner has taught me to walk*
> *and walk and resist*
> *I may offer my robe and my bed for sale*
> *I may work as stonemason, porter, street cleaner*
> *I may search cattle dung for a grain*
> *I may live naked and in hunger*
> *O enemies of the sun, but, I will not bargain*
> *To the last pulse in my veins I will resist*

Beside me, Asma' crouched, weapons in hand, her eyes crossing land and sky towards Ramallah, the land of her birth, seeing her father slaughtered before her eyes.

At the entrance to the cave sat Um Youssef in her white head-scarf, skin burnished by the sun like Aunt Bahiya, eyes gazing at the West Bank, covered by a solid layer of tears, unblinking as the canons boomed and the earth and sky merged in one mass of fire. She remained seated, waiting. Then I saw her jump up and run without stopping until she reached the river bank. She paced anxiously up and down like a mother who has lost her only child. Suddenly three young men appeared from the river carrying a wounded boy and she rushed towards them to help carry him. With a muslin bandage and cotton wool, she dressed the wound, then helped carry him to the jeep, which sped off to Salt Hospital.

In the hospital I saw her pass from one casualty to another, removing soiled bandages and putting on clean ones. I heard them call her 'our mother', as they called the land and home-land, and she called them 'my children', as she called the land planted with vegetation. She was not married, had neither house nor man, but all houses were her house, all men her men, the women her women, the young people hers. Her original name was Um Youssef and in her memory was a thirty-year-old love affair and a child named Youssef whose name alone she remembered as if he were a figment of her imagination or a child as yet unborn, or whom she had borne and lost on the West Bank.

As the ambulance was taking the wounded boy from the riverside, speeding us along the Jordan Valley on its way to Salt, I saw a shadow running behind us which had appeared from nowhere. After some minutes it became clear to me that there was a woman running behind the vehicle and I asked the driver to stop. The woman rushed up to the vehicle without talking or turning to us. She scrutinised the face of the wounded boy, then with delicate fingers began to examine his hands and feet.

A *feda'i* took hold of her gently and separated her from him, whispering to me sadly: She does not hear anyone or answer anyone. During the day she searches among the tents and at night she lies beside the river. When she notices an injured or drowned person, she gets up and runs to him, and examines his face and hands and feet as though looking for someone she knows.

I saw this woman a lot during the period I lived in Salt. Sometimes she ran behind the ambulance; sometimes I would see her kneeling among the rocks in the Jordan Valley, rummaging through the earth and eating dust. Once, I came face to face with her roaming amongst the tents. She looked up at me with large tear-filled eyes, a deep gash beneath one of them like the scar of Um Youssef. But she was not Um Youssef although she too looked like my Aunt Bahiya. Whilst her facial features were strong, her body seemed to melt into the light as if lost. Nobody knew her real name and they called her *Ain al-Hayya*, the source of life.

When I returned to Egypt, this woman with her deep-set eyes appeared to me in my sleep, waking me from the deepest slumber. I put pen to paper and drew her in the form of a story with her name as its title.

PART FOUR

The Women's Conference in Helsinki

It was my first trip to that cold region near the North Pole called Scandinavia, those countries squeezed between the eastern and western superpowers and separating them like an insulation barrier; cold, quiet and as still as a point on a string stretched between two equivalent forces.

This stillness is the dominant feature of these countries and their people. Even nature seems still, since night does not follow day nor does the day end with the coming of night. The sun stays in the sky, still and unmoving, neither setting nor falling over the horizon, its red glow remaining steady. The eye is confused, no longer knows whether it sees a real sky or an artist's painting.

After midnight, I returned to my small room in Valley Hotel in Helsinki. I could hardly tell day from night except for the natural tiredness the body feels when it is time for sleep. I drew the heavy curtain over the window to shut out the sunlight and to create night inside my room so I could sleep. It was June 1969; the white night of Finland lasts ninety nights in the summer and is countered by dark days in the winter when there is no day or sunlight, only permanent night for twenty-four hours.

The streets of Helsinki were clean and quiet. People's faces were clean and quiet, almost emotionless, with a curious stillness in their eyes, like wells of purity. But it was a cold purity, with the coldness of water that is stored in the belly of the earth.

But this was only the external Helsinki, the hard, icy layer on the surface of Finland's sea. If it was broken by modern Finnish boats or melted under the summer sun, the water gushed out from under it, warm and plentiful, to reveal the human nature of Finnish hearts that were no different from

67

others in other times and places. Even in politics, under that cold, neutral and unemotional layer, there was permanent conflict between eight political parties: the Conservatives, the Liberals, the Moderates, the Farmers, the Democratic Socialists, the Opposition party, the Democratic Finns and the Swedish minority.

The Democratic Socialist party corresponded to the Labour Party in Britain, whilst the Democratic Finns represented the far left. These two parties alone held half the parliamentary seats, the other half being held by the other six parties. No one party was in the majority. Despite the permanent conflict between representatives of the left and right, the balance was almost permanent and the government represented a group of parties, not just one.

Finland gained independence and declared itself an independent republic, emerging from under Czarist Russian domination in 1917, the same year Russia liberated itself from Czarist power and created the first socialist state in the Soviet Union under the leadership of Lenin.

Since the end of the Second World War and the signing of the peace treaty in Paris in 1947, Finland has declared its determination to be neutral and to remain outside the conflict between the superpowers.

In 1952 the Council of Scandinavian States was formed, comprising five states: Sweden, Norway, Denmark, Iceland and Finland. One social and political system has prevailed over this northern region of Europe, one passport, one stand in the United Nations . . . a cold and permanent stand of neutrality that is impassive, no matter how the world reacts or how intense the conflict between the superpowers.

That was the government position in 1969. As for the people, they were like any other people in the world. A Finnish woman said to me: We read a lot about the struggle of the Vietnamese people, the wars in the Middle East, about the Palestinian people expelled from their homeland . . . American imperialism is behind all this!

The quiet, outer layer disappeared and was replaced by reaction and discussion.

The conference was huge, all women, organised by the World

Democratic Union of Women; over one thousand women representing ninety-two countries and thirty or more representatives of international organisations. It was the first time in my life that I spent five whole days in the company of women of all nationalities.

I sat in one of the seats reserved for the Egyptian delegation. I did not pin on a badge, for since childhood I have hated badges on women's chests. The windows in the hall closed, the artificial air-conditioned air mixing in my chest with the smell of perfume. The words of the heads of delegations on the platform pounded in my head like hammer blows.

I sneezed aloud to expel the artificial air and words. The head of the Egyptian delegation heard me sneeze and threw me a sharp look from the platform. Noticing I wore no badge, she thought I was against the regime. After getting down from the platform, she found herself sitting beside a woman from Israel. She jumped up, startled, gathered up her papers and rushed down the passageway between the seats to sit somewhere else. Other members of the delegation followed, waddling along behind her on their spiky high heels like a slow flock of ducks.

I remained where I was. There were more than two meters between myself and the Israeli woman, my back towards her and my eyes on the platform, but for the head of the delegation it was as if I had made a peace treaty with Israel.

The Vietnamese issue took precedence in the delegates' speeches. All of them joined in condemning American policy and hostility against the Vietnamese people. A young woman guerrilla from Vietnam, called Wanto Anto, stood on the platform dressed in khaki, her wide eyes raised upward. She was no more than twenty-four years old and had led a company in South Vietnam. She had lost her sister in the war and her brother had been held captive for nine years while she was fighting. Under her leadership, her company had managed to shoot down an American plane, burn a boat and kill two hundred American soldiers. She alone had killed thirty-five American soldiers. Her body was as small as a child's, her plaits as long as a schoolgirl's and her smile as gentle as a mother's. She herself was the mother of an eight-month-old child, but the sharp look in her eyes and her rapid steps, like the pounce of a cheetah, assured me that she could kill.

After Vietnam, came the Palestinian issue. The Palestinian delegate stood on the platform. She told us the history of the establishment of Israel; of Israeli, English and American war weapons; of the Palestinian people killed by the thousand; of their expulsion from their land to live in camps outside the homeland; of their subjugation and humiliation in the occupied territories inside Israel.

The Palestinian cause got the support of all the delegations apart from those of Romania and Israel.

I saw her for the first time as she was sitting in the midst of a group of women. Her face was familiar and I wondered where I'd seen her before. In an instant I recognised her . . . it was Valentina, whose picture had appeared in the newspapers after she returned to earth from a flight in a spaceship and was awarded the golden star. She headed the Soviet delegation to the conference. A slim young woman with delicate features, a straight pointed nose, deep blue eyes, thin closed lips which rarely opened despite the quiet, natural smile which spread over the features of her small face. Women from different delegations gathered around to embrace her, showering her with expressions of admiration and questions: How did you take off into the sky? Were you afraid? The whole world recognises your heroism; do you feel yourself to be great? You are beautiful and delicate, how did you carry out such a fantastic journey? One of the women embraced her and exclaimed:

– I never thought that one day I would see you with my very own eyes. I never imagined you to be a woman of flesh and blood like the rest of us.

Despite this heady atmosphere of adulation, Valentina showed no sign of conceit. She remained quietly smiling and in the flood of admiration, did not forget the other members of the Soviet delegation. She presented them one by one to the women, saying quietly: I am not alone. We have heroines all over the Soviet Union who struggle each day in order to build a new society.

Valentina talked only for a few minutes, then handed over to her comrades on the delegation. They all took part in the talk and discussion.

On the last day of the conference, final declarations and resolutions were issued and the following paper was distributed:

To all mothers and women of the world.
We came to Helsinki, representing millions of women in different countries, to study the role of women in today's world. Women in the past dedicated their lives to housework but today they participate in everything that happens in the world and in everything concerning their countries' problems. They have realised that the solution to these problems is inseparably linked to achieving national independence, freedom and peace, and to their obtaining their cultural, social, economic and political rights. In their struggle for liberation, for equality with men, for a better life in the family, in society and at work, women represent a progressive force against backwardness and exploitation. Although we represent countries that differs politically, that belong to different societies and beliefs, we all agree that the world faces a threat that demands all our efforts and solidarity. We condemn the monstrous war waged by world colonialism and imperialism against the Vietnamese people, in Laos, in Korea and in the Middle East. We condemn Israel and world imperialism that supports it in its aggression against the Arab countries. Over two million Palestinian refugees have been expelled from their country and we support their right to resist aggression and to return to their homeland. We call for the restoration of the rights of the Palestinian people and support the armed struggle of the Arab peoples against aggression and demand the withdrawal of all Israeli forces from occupied Arab territories and the implementation of the Security Council resolutions of 22 November 1967.
We support the struggle of the African peoples in their war against new and old colonialism and support

the struggle of the people of Angola, Mozambique and Portuguese Guinea against Portuguese colonialism, and the struggle of the people of South Africa and Rhodesia against the fascist and racist regimes in their countries. We support the struggle of the Cuban people against military, political and economic pressures. We support the struggle of any people in the world for independence, freedom and peace. We support the people of Greece, Spain and Portugal, and the people of Latin America against any fascist, dictatorial power. We support any movement fighting against racial discrimination in America and anywhere in the world. We condemn American imperialism as the power behind all aggression and wars in the world, as the force behind military pacts with its bases spread throughout Asia, Africa, Australia and Europe. It is fundamentally responsible for the arms race which consumes millions of dollars and the immense human potential that the world desperately needs to eliminate hunger, disease, poverty and ignorance.

One of the Finnish women called Natasha, a member of the Finnish–Arab Friendship Society, invited me to supper in her house. We drove in her small car around the clean streets of Helsinki, passing green forests and lakes as pure as distilled water. Finally we reached her house set among trees and water. I stood looking out from the balcony, the night air cool and refreshing. A night ray fell on the surface of the still lake, a strange white ray which confused the eye so you hardly knew whether it was the sun or the moon that lit up the universe. But it was the sun in the night sky.

I wandered through Natasha's spacious apartment filled with quiet and silence.
– Do you live alone?
– With my son.
– And your husband?
– I am not married.
I was silent for a moment, then said: Is that usual here?
– Yes.

– And your son. How does society regard him?

– Like any other boy. He carries my name and that's something to be proud of, as I have a successful job.

– Don't you have any problems with illegitimate children?

– No, we don't. Every child that's born is legitimate.

– Why aren't you married?

– I loved him and wanted to marry him, but he didn't want to marry me.

– Haven't you met a man who did want to marry you?

– Yes, some, but I didn't love them.

– You would not agree to marriage unless you were in love?

– Of course not.

– Are you in love now?

She looked at me and said:

– Have you found a contradiction between my personality as you knew it at the conference and my private life? Here, we separate work from private life. When I work, I give myself to work, and when I rest I give myself to rest and pleasure. As to the question of marrying or not marrying, that's something I can't determine alone, but only with a man . . . Now let me ask you something frankly – what would you do if you loved a man and he refused to marry you? Doesn't that happen sometimes in your country?

– It often happens.

– What does the woman do in that case?

– It's hard to explain. But does such freedom exist in all Scandinavian countries?

– Of course, but I think that Finnish women are more advanced than others. Maybe it's cultural, but history proves it. Finnish women were the first in Europe to obtain political rights in 1906.

On the last night in Helsinki I did not sleep. In one hour I would leave Finland with a group of women for my first trip to the Soviet Union. I should have returned to Cairo after the Helsinki conference ended, but Valentina the astronaut had invited us to visit her country. I had only ever seen Russia before in novels and in the cinema. In my mind, the Soviet Union was contradictory images, some as bright as sunlight, others as dark as the other side of the moon.

I had heard the word 'socialism' for the first time when I was ten years old. When I entered secondary school, I met a slim, brown girl called Su'ad who gave me a newspaper called *al-Gamahir* (The Masses), and in medical school I met a student named Yusri who passed me a paper entitled *al-Gami'a* (The Public). Yusri was nicknamed 'The Red Student' by the other students.

Before graduating from medical school, I read Tolstoy and Dostoevsky and Marx and Engels and Lenin and Krovskaya and Pushkin and Gorky and Turgenev. Dostoevsky was closer to me than Tolstoy, Friedrich Engels and Krovskaya closer than Karl Marx and Lenin.

From my balcony in Helsinki I stood looking at the last white night as it drew to an end, just as surprised as on the first night in Finland. The white night slips into white day so that the two are barely distinguishable, other than by the movement of cars and the appearance of people on the street.

In my imagination, the Soviet Union was as light and white as the summer nights in Finland. But it was also like the silent night which remains immersed in a mysterious stillness.

PART FIVE

First
Journey
to the
Red World

We took the train from Helsinki to Leningrad, four women to a coach, in each coach four bunks, two of them on the upper level onto which a fat woman could not jump. Bahija from Afghanistan took one of them, whilst I took the other.

– You're very slim, said Bahija. Are you married?

– Yes, I said, three times, and I've got two children. And you?

– I have seven children from two husbands, she replied.

She laughed, was silent for a while, then with sadness in her voice said: We are destroying the antiquated values of our society in order to build a new one in which people can enjoy justice. People cannot be at peace whilst they are ruled by force. They may appear to be at peace but beneath the surface you'll find revolution.

Hearing a noise in the corridor, we rushed outside to see Rosa the Argentinian holding a guitar and singing in Spanish: *I am a prisoner breaking my chains, going out into the open.* Latin American women sat around her on the floor echoing the refrains of the song with her. The singing was infectious and each group of women began to sing in their own language. The Arab women sang a popular nationalist song, *Wallah Zamaan YaSilahi*, the Soviet women sang *Katyusha*, Oketa and Wanto Anto sang the Vietnamese people's anthem; the black American woman, Shirley, sang *My face is black but my heart is white*.

The singing of the women drowned out the sound of the train, voices and songs in different languages and accents rang through the air, Arab tunes mixed with Russian, Afghani

77

with American, with Spanish, with English, with French, with Vietnamese. I found myself singing a song, the words and language of which I did not know. We became one group, from one country, and the artificial differences that separate people from each other disappeared.

Valentina the astronaut sat with us. She had a small bunk like those of other women in the third class of the train. Looking at her face, I was surprised by the natural simplicity of her quiet features.

Then we heard a voice over the microphone announce that we had crossed the borders of Finland and were on Soviet soil. I put my head out of the train window to look and saw trees, land, houses, and every person in the street or field or house. Despite the movement of the train I examined them closely, looking at clothes and shoes. Why shoes in particular? But how many rumours I'd heard!

Everything seemed normal – the land was like land, the trees like trees, the people like people, and had it not been for the voice announcing that we had crossed the border, I'd have thought we were still in Finland.

I went back to bed to sleep a little, then awoke suddenly to the sound of the train stopping. And now I began to feel I was in the Soviet Union. The station platform was full of men and women and children carrying flowers, welcoming the women's delegations and crowding around Valentina. I scrutinised them; they wore beautiful and elegant clothes, there was vigour in their faces and a sparkle in their eyes; I was drawn to the lively faces of the children. These were villagers from Lojika, the first Soviet village on the border. The women's delegations walked, showered with greetings and flowers, to the spacious station restroom where tables had been laid. Valentina sat amongst us. The corks of champagne bottles began popping and flying through the air, together with laughter and jokes. Women from all countries of the world ate Russian caviar, chicken meat and together drank toasts to friendship, freedom and peace.

The train brought us into Leningrad in the middle of the night, but the sun was still in the sky, illuminating the large city with white day light. In the white light, the burnished copper domes glowed and the large buildings were reflected on the surface of the River Neva which flowed under the bridges into the Finnish Gulf.

Beyond the river shone the copper dome of a huge building plunged into silence. It was one of the old prisons; in one of its cells Dostoyevsky had lived for a period; Maxim Gorky had also been inside this prison before the socialist revolution and had lived within its walls, writing. Facing the prison on the near side of the river was his towering statue, cap in hand, and not far away stood Lenin with his fine features, medium height, hand raised towards the white hall, the first hall in Russia to witness the revolution of peasants and workers. On the wooden chairs, besides the chairs and on the windows had sat the workers and peasants on 26 October 1917; Lenin had entered the hall with his rapid steps and declared the first socialist state in the history of Russia.

We were taken to visit factories. One of them was a red flag factory, said to be one of the largest cloth factories in the Soviet Union. Of the ten thousand workers, eighty-five per cent were women. The manager was an elegant young woman who introduced us to a group, saying: This is the secretary of the Party committee in the factory; this is the convenor of the youth committee; this is the head of the union committee. Young women sat with us around a table covered with flowers and bottles of mineral water and champagne and platters of black and red caviar, fish and meat. We had to drink toasts to the factory and the workers.

As we walked around the enormous factory, the women workers greeted us with smiles and pinned badges and stars on us. They worked eight hours a day with two days' holiday a week. The minimum wage for male and female workers was 110 rubles a month, the maximum 200 rubles, according to production and skill. The factory manager took 300 rubles a month. In the factory were six crèches for the workers' children from the ages of two months to seven years. Every woman had the right to maternity leave for a period of twelve whole months, four of them fully waged; two before the birth and two after. In the factory was a summer camp for children and camps for young people from the ages of seven to twenty-eight years. There was also a rest clinic and hospital. A doctor's wage was 180 rubles a month, a nurse's 100 rubles.

In the middle of the large square outside was a flame in front of a monument to the unknown soldier and the graves of 700,000 martyrs. The women's delegations filed by, followed by hundreds of tourists from all over the world who carried flowers and walked to the music of Tchaikovsky that played quietly and contained a little sadness and a lot of strength. White and red flowers piled up at the feet of the unknown soldier, where these words were written in Russian:

'We will not forget your courage or patience. We will not forget the winter of oppression and the bombs of 1943. We will not forget you and we will not surrender.'

A Russian friend of mine, Nina, said: The people of Leningrad resisted heroically for 900 days in the face of the Nazi siege. Leningrad lived through the war against the Nazis from 1941 to 1945 during which a million martyrs died and the whole city was bombarded with bombs and artillery. But look how Leningrad has re-emerged! That's the people's determination for freedom!

I had never seen a country with such a passion for museums as the Soviet Union. Leningrad alone has fifty museums. Everything there that has a relationship to history or to artists has been turned into a museum. Artists enjoy an esteem that verges on veneration. The houses of writers and poets have been turned into museums, statues of them erected, squares named after them. Near Leningrad is the town of Pushkin, the statue of Pushkin in the centre – even the youngest child knew Pushkin's poetry.

You have to spend a whole day at the Hermitage Museum and even then you cannot see all the paintings. It would take eighty years to see all the paintings at the Hermitage if you went every day for seven hours a day. And then you could only see every painting in the museum if you stood in front of each one for a minute only, there are so many!

I did not try to begin the experiment.

I have never seen a party such as the Carnival of the White Night. The garden of the Summer Palace in Leningrad was turned into a carnival on the morning of 22 November. The

Summer Palace, now a museum, was one of the palaces of the Russian Czar before the revolution. I have seen palaces in different countries, but as soon as I entered the Russian Czar's palace I understood the reasons for the socialist revolution in Russia.

The palace gardens were like a dream of trees and greenery and flowers and aromatic plants and vines under which ran brooks and streams, statues of gold, golden domes from the tops of which spouted innumerable water fountains. On a marble platform in the midst of the fountains, the Leningrad ballet troupe danced *Swan Lake*. The ballerinas danced amongst the fountains in their white dresses like birds of paradise or the genii of legends and stories. A statue of Samson stood in one corner of the garden surrounded by fountains, a statue of Adam and the Apple surrounded by birds of paradise. Thousands of men, women and children came from all corners of the Soviet Union and from all countries of the world to watch the Carnival of the White Night, carrying flowers and dancing to the music that arose from all corners of the garden, faces radiating a vitality that infected all who saw them. I looked about in amazement. Was this all a dream?

The boat was called Turgenev after the well-known Russian writer, and the river was the Volga, the most famous river in the Soviet Union. They call it the river of revolution, love and melodies. It is the river which crosses the Tartar Republic where Lenin grew up. Lenin's family lived in a small Tartar town on the Volga and which is now named Ulyanovsk after his family.

The Volga at Ulyanovsk, where the boat brought us, was wide and we could no longer see the other bank. We were told that it was forty kilometers wide in this area. The rain was pouring down; the weather changed suddenly and it grew extremely cold. Despite this, we saw the people of Ulyanovsk waiting for us on the riverside carrying umbrellas and flowers while music played. I never imagined that the Soviet people would be so warm and emotional or that women enjoyed such status amongst the Tartars.

As happened at every reception champagne corks flew

through the air, the women ate caviar, fish and meat and everyone drank toasts. We drank to the head chef and his comrades who had made the food we ate. Yunis Ahmed, the head chef (the Tartars are Muslim and their names are Arabic), raised his glass and replied to the toast, then sat down at his table beside the Tartar deputy prime minister, ministers and Party members. After the food, everyone stood up to sing the national anthem. Then the music began playing and everyone broke into dancing and singing. I saw the deputy prime minister play the piano, the social security minister dance, the education minister join in a ring of dancing women. Nothing seemed unnatural, no one seemed to differ from each other, everyone was relaxed and looked contented.

We walked through the streets of Ulyanovsk to a small wooden house. We had to put on cloth slippers over our own shoes, a system followed before entering any museum, to protect the floor from the millions of heels that come from all over the world. I climbed the wooden staircase that led to Lenin's bedroom, a little doorless room directly off the stairs with a small metal bed; beside it was a table on which were books protected by glass. The titles of the books read: *Das Capital, The History of Marxism in Russia, The Origins of the Family* by Friedrich Engels, and other books on law, economics and philosophy.

We toured the small house, listening to the commentary of the Russian translator. Lenin died in 1924 but he remains alive throughout the Soviet Union. His statues are in every village and town, his words are engraved in stone, his books and words are practically memorised by heart. Even his corpse is unburied and has not turned to dust like other human bodies, but has remained preserved in his tomb in Red Square in Moscow.

We went on to Maxim Gorky Street, and Gorky Museum, then took a large boat along the Volga. Zouba, a member of the Soviet Women's Union, sang the Russian song *The Volga Boatmen*. Some refrains of the song are like the song of the Nile, *heila hop heila*. We all joined in the singing. The weather had begun to clear, the sun shone and the women took off their coats and winter clothes and put on spring and summer ones.

*

In Moscow, in the vast vestibule of the Hotel Russia, I met a number of Egyptian and Arab writers on their way to a writers' conference in Tashkent, and later received a bouquet of flowers and a letter of invitation to the Tashkent conference. I left the women's delegation and found myself and my luggage on the writers' plane. We flew from Moscow to the capital of Kazakhstan in five and a half hours. Getting off the plane at the airport, a hot summer breeze, like that of an Egyptian summer seared our faces. The people of Kazakhstan have snub noses and slanting eyes like Chinese people. All that separates them from China is a range of snow-capped mountains on the slopes of which grow trees, vegetables and fruit. They cultivate the mountains here and make artificial rivers and lakes from the melting snow on the peaks. They divert the course of natural rivers to a high dam that generates electricity. The people of Kazakhstan sent their experts to Sudan and helped the Egyptians build the Aswan High Dam.

The president of the Writers' Union headed the delegation that met us at the airport with flowers. We drank to friendship between the people of Asia and Africa and toasted our children already born and those as yet unborn. They love children and, instead of limiting the birthrate, give rewards to mothers after their fourth child.

The laughter and chatter grew louder as the formality between Indian, Egyptian, Algerian, Sudanese, Russian and African writers disappeared and we all became people of the same country, the country of art and literature.

On the table was a large jug full of milk. Yuri Brovitz, president of the Moscow Writers' Union, poured me a glass. As I took a sip, my throat burned with acid.

Yuri laughed: It's horse milk . . . very healthy, five per cent alcohol.

– Do you really drink mare's milk? I asked.

– Do you really drink cow's milk? he replied.

What is the difference between mare's milk and cow's milk?

I took a piece of grilled meat from a plate that tasted delicious. I said to my neighbour Laria, the Russian translator: Delicious meat.

— Very, she said. It's horse meat.

I hid my surprise. Hands holding glasses of mare's milk were raised in toast to art and friendship, so I raised mine too and drank.

A car took us up the winding roads of the mountain they call the Green Peak. Streams of melted snow from the summit meandered through trees and vegetation. When the car stopped somewhere on the mountain, a group of farmers came to meet us and were introduced by the president of the collective farmers. The men were wearing suits. They took us to a farmhouse where, as usual, we saw a long table spread with food. Nearby was a swimming pool. In such hot weather the water was so tempting that some of the writers dived in for a swim, then stretched out under the sun.

We toured the farm with the farmers. Our guide told us:

We are building a socialist person with new values on the basis of collective work, cooperation with others and making a living in proportion to work and production. The individual is secure in his and his children's future, is not anxious or fearful of illness, disability or old age. The state takes care of all that. We do not have to worry about our children's education and expenses since the state has lifted this burden from us. Everything is provided equally for our children.

A woman is like a man here, working in any job, driving tractors and agricultural machinery, taking her due of the wages. She has the same political and social rights as a man. We do not have a problem of illegitimate children. Every child that's born is legitimate, and takes the name of father or mother, with all rights. People here marry for love; family links are strong and divorce is not easy but requires certain procedures and rules. Lenin is the founder of socialism in our country but he was not alone. Many of our people were heroes with him. We do not like the cult of the individual, whoever he was, and we dislike those who worship Lenin or Marx. We want to liberate people from the rituals of slavery. Here we have freedom of opinion within a Marxist-Leninist framework. We don't want free thought, no matter what the framework. We have eliminated ignorance, superstition and illiteracy, and have become the second state in the world after only fifty years. We have achieved socialism in our society, but we are still very far from communism and have many years to go yet. We will only reach communism after achieving a surplus in our material potential and changing people's ways of thinking so that the principle, 'from each according to his ability to each according to his need', can be put into practice. Changing people's thinking is the hardest thing of all.

We flew in a four-propellor plane to Tashkent, the capital of Kazakhstan. The weather was clear and warm, the sun like the Egyptian sun. The people's features, too, were similar to Egyptian ones, with some of the customs and characteristics of Muslims; in their collective farms, the peasants wore skull caps like Arabs. Were it not that the language differed, I'd have thought myself in Egypt. We toured the town museums and statues, went to concert halls, libraries, theatres, research institutes, factories, kindergartens, hospitals, children's and youth camps. The guide told us that they had planted the mountains with forests, extracted minerals from the earth and that in only two years' time, Uzbekistan alone would produce eighty per cent of the Soviet Union's gold. They had introduced innovative methods in agriculture, made artificial rain in some collective farms and produced new types of fruit. They now had 1200 types of grapes alone, twenty-six institutes for fruit research and produced all types of drinks and wine.

They took us to a table of food set up by the sea shore. It was like the shore at Alexandria and I could not see the other side, even staring hard. But it was a sea without waves, like Lake Qaroun in Fayoum. They told us that it was one of the artificial lakes of Uzbekistan. Some of the writers put on swimsuits and dived into the water. The Soviet writer, Sovronov, leaned on his wife's shoulder and together they sang songs of Moscow. Natasha danced a Tashkent folk dance. The Indian author Malik Raj Ananid took Larisa's hand and began reading her palm. I overheard part of their conversation:
– What do you see in my palm, Doctor Malik?
– You have a husband whom you love and two children.
– I've told you that many times before.

– In general, the lines of your palm confirm that you've told me the truth.

– What about my future in literature?

– Your heart line shows that your heart is pure. Your heart is pure, Larisa, too pure to understand the evils of life. For this reason, you will never become a writer.

The Sudanese writer Mohammed Suleiman was talking passionately to the Russian translator about the Sudanese revolution.

The Algerian author Mawloud Mamri had forgotten his swimsuit in the hotel and stood staring at the water for a long time. Then he threw himself into the sea fully clothed. Yuri Petrovitch was holding a skewer of hot kebab which he ate with relish; then he rose at the head of the table and asked everyone to drink to Arab–Soviet friendship. Everybody rushed to raise their glasses and a Tashkent poet recited some verses in the Uzbekistani language.

On the way back, a soft melody emerged from somewhere, and beside the road were trees, streams of water, lakes in which children swam, buildings, paths. Before the coach brought us into the town, I saw a woman driving a steamroller, tarring the road. When I waved to her through the window, she drove nearer. I saw her exhausted face scorched by the sun and drenched in sweat. I heard her say something angrily. Larisa translated her words.

The woman had said: You don't have to look at me, you tourists, like a bull in a zoo and don't believe that women here are equal to men. I work in the street and at home too.

I flew to Moscow. I hadn't seen it yet. Maybe that was upside down, since people enter a house through its door and enter a country through its capital. But you can enter a house through the window.

I pulled the curtain back from the high window on the top floor of the vast Hotel Russia and there was Red Square before my eyes. The golden domes of the Kremlin were topped by a shining red star. The old deserted church was wrapped in scaffolding and was being renovated in preparation for Lenin's Centenary celebrations. Facing the church stood Lenin's square red mausoleum and behind it, adjacent to the Kremlin walls, the tombs of the martyrs. Behind the high wall of the Kremlin, the Moscow river flowed silently, apart from a soft melody which I could hardly hear. Although I was exhausted, I felt an urge to walk the streets of Moscow at night. A Russian friend named Vera whom I'd met, learned of my desire to walk.

We crossed Red Square and walked along the river. The night was warm. Flocks of young people swayed to the rhythm of the quiet night, in couples or in small groups, humming or singing or holding onto each other and dancing to old Russian melodies. On the wooden bench beside the river, boys and girls exchanged embraces and kisses. Young people are the same all over the world – nothing can come between them and embraces and kisses.

The last day of the trip arrived. Vera suggested that I visit Lenin's tomb. Every day I saw the long queue in Red Square, the guards in their uniforms walking with slow steps, saluting on the hour. Since childhood, I have hated military and civil rituals. The movement of the body appears to me mechanical. And I hate even more the sight of soldiers standing motionless like lampposts. But that morning, I went down from my room into the large reception hall, then walked to Red Square. The queue in front of the mausoleum was long and I considered re-turning to the hotel, but curiosity made me wait. There must be something worth seeing here since these waves of people came every day and waited for hours to enter.

The queue moved very slowly, the July sun above our heads. No one left their place in the line. It was like the queue on the Day of Judgement walking along a straight path. The fires of hell were not beneath our feet but rather above our heads. And above them the domes of the Kremlin, topped by the red star.

Finally, I found myself on the threshold of the mausoleum. A cool breeze brushed my face. I walked slowly behind the others. I saw Lenin lying inside a glass room, the soft red light that fell on his face hiding the paleness of his skin and giving it an artificial rose colour. All eyes turned towards him in awe, like silent prayer.

A shiver ran through my body, like the first time I entered

the operating theatre in college and saw a corpse, like the first time I saw a mummy embalmed in an old sarcophagus.

– Embalming is a science the ancient Egyptians knew five thousand years ago, I said.

– Lenin was great, Vera replied.

– Yes, I said. But I hate paganism and the worship of embalmed bodies.

PART SIX

*Iran
Before the
Revolution*

My first trip to Iran in November 1968 was a scientific medical one within the confines of Teheran University. I sat amongst members of the doctors' convention, their names and titles pinned to their chests, listening to long repetitious papers on health and sickness. Then I left the university and took a taxi along one straight road to my small room in the hotel. I find such an exclusively scientific life unbearable, especially when I'm abroad, for science is not my sole objective when I travel. 'Science' can be found in Egyptian universities or in libraries or at home; one does not have to travel to another country and sit within the confines of its university in order to study science. As for knowledge, that is something other than science and, above all, entails escaping from universities and libraries to life, people and the streets. This is the great importance of travel.

I managed to find a way of escaping – through literature. Literature in my life is unlike literature in the lives of those official authors who write and get paid and eat, drink and travel abroad in order to write. For me, literature is something unofficial, something unacceptable for a doctor. I write at night after I've finished my official tasks like sinful love, to relieve myself of the pressures of my legitimate life.

Thus I found myself collecting together my pens, books and notes and very quietly leaving the lecture theatre. I went out into the university courtyard. The November sun was warm; Iranian students were dotted around the courtyard, their faces not very different from ours. The pronounced eastern features of the boys had a certain heaviness and eastern masculinity that did not match their shoulder-length hair. And the girls with their light, wheat-coloured skin, their large doe-like eyes full of shy apprehension, were not yet liberated from servile feminine complexes despite the American eye make-up and the miniskirts that revealed ample eastern thighs.

In the middle of the courtyard was a beautiful, well-ordered garden centred by a fountain that filled a basin as large as a swimming pool and reflected the golden sunlight. Around it, young men and women sat and whispered to each other, eyes sparkling and burning with youthful love and desire. But traditions still forbade embracing and kissing in front of others. Facing this dreamlike garden was a huge sedate mosque, its white walls decorated with verses from the *Quran*. From its round minaret came a voice in Arabic calling people to afternoon prayer.

I did not know exactly where I was going, but saw a large building facing this mosque, on which was written 'Faculty of Literature' in Farsi. I told myself this was perhaps the door to Farsi literature. I went in and asked for the best author in Iran and was told that he was the dean of the college, so I bought a new notebook and went to meet him in his sumptuous office. I sat with him for half an hour and wrote down not one word in my book on literature. Then I left hurriedly through the back door of the university, so avoiding the carriage which lay in wait for me after lectures to carry me like a valuable charge to the hotel.

As it had begun to pour, I went into a small restaurant from which the aroma of 'shilo kebab' wafted. The tables were packed with men and women, in front of them plates as big as trays laden with skewers of various types of *kufta* made from greens and vegetables and lamb, Iranian bread as large as pancakes, onions and red turnip. I sat next to a group of young people unlike those I had seen at the university. Their features were coarser, their hair cut short, in their eyes a look that contained bitterness and anger. I love such looks in people, as if, in my view, they were created in order to rebel and be angry. Or perhaps this is a view that a lifetime of bitterness, anger and revolution have created for me.

Amongst them was a girl called Mani, with short black hair and shining black eyes. I found myself joining in their conversation. Fortunately, they knew a bit of English and I had learned a few words of Farsi. Talking to them I discovered the way to the real Iran, the real Iranian youth. I also learned how to contact the leading Iranian author whose books the people snatched up and whose words they memorised whilst waiting for his new works.

The way to reach him was long and tortuous. Unlike other famous people, he did not live in the heart of the capital, Teheran, but in a distant area north of Teheran called Shami-ran. The road there climbed up into the mountains. On either side were tall trees and canals in which rain water and melted snow from the mountains ran. The towering white peaks pierced the sky and reflected the golden rays of the sun.

The car brought me to a narrow street, then entered an alley and stopped in front of a small old house. A young man with white hair came out. His features were immediately familiar, as though I'd seen him before, which is always what happens when I meet a person of this sort. He was wearing simple clothes. His house inside and out was simple. His small car, so old it looked as if it couldn't move, stood in front of the narrow entrance to the house. It was perhaps the first old car I'd seen in Teheran where new American cars crowded the streets and squares.

An invisible aura surrounds some people; they give off an energy that has an extraordinary radiation, perhaps from the mind or from the soul or from something deep inside, which we strangers respond to with something equally deep and unknown inside us.

His name was Jalal al-Ahmed. People in Iran knew him and read his books, but the Shah's government confiscated them and banned his new manuscripts. His students and readers smuggled them out of Iran and published them in other countries, then they distributed them secretly in Iran. There was a leanness about him that gave his face an air of exhaustion, as though he neither slept nor ate. His features were thoroughly Iranian, the skin sunburnt, the nose straight and sharp, and his large, black eyes had a frank and open look. He had written a long novel entitled *The Curse of the Earth* which described the tragedy of the *fellahin* in Iran, and a book called *Down with the West* in which he attacked western imperialism. This book had been banned in Iran, but the students of Jalal Al Ahmed published it in California and secretly distributed fifty thousand copies of it in Iran.

– I make the job easier for my students, Jalal Al Ahmed said, by writing on the sleeve that the book may be freely printed anywhere and at any time without restriction or conditions and without any rights to the author, so what's printed is printed and what's distributed is distributed.

He had written works on the Palestinian issue, the latest of which was a small booklet that he wrote after the war of 5 June 1967. But the authorities in Iran had confiscated that and burned down the publishing house that published it. Some of his students had smuggled it out of the country and published it; it was translated into Arabic and distributed in Beirut.

We sat in the small garden of his house. His wife, Dr Simin Danshwar, joined us. She was a professor at Teheran University and had also written books and a collection of stories entitled *The Extinguished Fire*. She had kept her father's name, Danshwar, and had not taken that of her husband, Jalal Al Ahmed. Her features were like those of Egyptian women. The atmosphere was so familiar I felt as though I was at home in Egypt. Simin put a tray of food and hot tea in front of us.

Jalal Al Ahmed took a pen and paper and drew a map of Iran and the Arabian Gulf. At a point on the Gulf he wrote 'Abadan' and at another point lower down, at its narrow neck, he wrote 'Massandam'. Beside it he wrote '1000 tons of oil'. Then Ahmed took one of his books and began turning the pages with long thin fingers. He stopped at some lines under which he drew a thick line.

He muttered something in Farsi, then said sadly:

– In other words, ninety per cent of Israel's oil comes from Abadan in our country! It's shameful, disgraceful!

I looked at him in silence for a while, then said:

– How can you live in Iran with such dangerous ideas?

Quietly, he replied:

– I live here because I'm not alone. With me is a large group of young people and writers that meet every week in a small café. I've been sacked from my job three times, but I'm not a civil servant, I'm a writer and an artist.

– What are you writing now? I asked him.

– I've just finished a new 400-page study on Israel that has taken years.

– Will you publish it here?

– If I can.

– And if you can't?

– My students will publish it abroad, like my other works.

The sun had set and it had grown dark without me knowing. I got up, stuffing Jalal Al Ahmed's Farsi writings into my bag. He and his wife, Simin Danshwar, saw me to the outer gate of the small garden. He held my hand and shook it, saying:

– Be sure that this regime in Iran will soon fall. Eighty per cent of the Iranian people live in the shadow of poverty, but this will not go on much longer. The Egyptian people and the Iranian people are friends. We love the Arabs, and Israel is our enemy too.

He stood before me, holding open the door. The sun had set and I noticed a black shadow move in the darkness. I turned round, and shivered.

Jalal Al Ahmed said wearily: The Shah's secret service is everywhere.

I held his hand firmly, filled with a strange misgiving, and found myself saying to him: Take care. You're surrounded by danger.

– Some of my friends have disappeared, he said quietly. My turn may come at any time.

I did not know, as I said goodbye, that it was a final goodbye – that I would visit Teheran two years later and not find him.

Returning alone on the dark road, I felt frightened. Drops of rain on the asphalt were like footsteps behind me. The rustle of the trees on the roadside coming down from the mountains was like the breathing of hidden ghosts. The darkness was dense, the mountains tall and black, the road narrow and winding to the bottom. When I reached my room in the hotel, I was drenched in sweat.

*

Two years later, in June 1970, I went to Teheran to attend a medical conference on birth control. Travelling with me was another doctor who worked in family planning called Doctor Surour. We bought tickets, then went to the Iranian Embassy in Cairo and filled in applications for entry visas to Teheran.

Dr Surour got an entry visa, but I did not. An official at the embassy told me:

– The authorities in Teheran have refused to give you a visa.

– Why? I asked in surprise.

– I don't know, the official said. The refusal came without any explanation.

I left the Iranian Embassy sadly. I wanted to travel to Iran again, to walk up that mountain road to Shamiran, along the narrow alley to the old house with the small garden, to talk long into the night with Jalal Al Ahmed and Simin Danshwar.

At the embassy door, I heard a voice behind me. I saw a tall, slender young man, with white hair like Jalal Al Ahmed.

– I read your article in *al-Musawwar* magazine two years ago, he said. The Shah's secret police wrote a report against it.

– What article? I asked.

– Your article about Jalal Al Ahmed that was published in *al-Musawwar*, number 2309, on 10 January 1969.

I was surprised that he had memorised the issue number and the date of publication, even though it had been two years ago. I myself had forgotten the article. I do not remember the articles I have written.

– Who are you? I asked. Do you work for the Iranian secret police?

He smiled: No, I work in the embassy press office. I liked your article and I loved Jalal Al Ahmed. He was my favourite author. I was very upset by his death.

– Death? I was shocked.

– Yes, he said quietly.

The same old shiver ran through my body. I saw Jalal Al Ahmed standing at the door, the black shadow in the darkness behind me, as though following me.

In the morning, I told Doctor Surour what had happened. He laughed with the scorn of doctors and said:

– You are a doctor, so why do you write and bring troubles on yourself? This one article has banned you from travelling to Teheran and from attending an important international conference.

His eyes behind his glasses were the eyes of a doctor, the gleam without depth or feeling. He knew nothing about life other than disease and germs. For him, people were either ill or would be ill before they died and in either event, ill or dead, he would get his price sooner or later.

His eyes glinted like glass and he never stopped looking at his watch. In his hand was a leather case that held a stethoscope, a blood pressure gauge, syringe and needle and an inner bag from which came the smell of iodine and blood.

Ever since I entered medical college, I've hated doctors. Their self-important walk along the corridors, the click of their metal heels on the tiles, their noses turned up away from the smell of wounds, their eyes fixed on the pockets of the sick, their metallic voices on platforms talking about humanity and compassion.

The voice of Doctor Surour was still in my ears, its scornful tone confirming my failure. I ran from the company of doctors to the company of writers, but found there no comfort, for in our country writers worked in journalism and were paid by the state like government officials, obeying orders from on high, their eyes on the rulers, their backs to the people and to humanity.

Since childhood, deep inside I've had the desire to defy orders. I found myself preparing my luggage. The conference was an international medical one; a decision had been issued on my travelling. I found conference papers from Geneva and on the bottom of one of them was written in English: *Should a member of the conference not obtain an entry visa to Teheran because of lack of time, he may obtain one on arrival at Teheran Airport.*

I walked towards the aeroplane with a heavy heart. I might get to Teheran only to return on the same plane to Cairo. Perhaps the Iranian Embassy had sent a telegram to Teheran Airport to prevent my entry. Maybe they would allow me to enter, then take revenge on me in Teheran. My mind spun with conflicting ideas, but my feet moved unswervingly towards the aeroplane. The face of Jalal Al Ahmed was before me. I did not believe he was dead: he was a young man, so how did he die? In what mysterious circumstances?

The plane rose into the sky and everything became white and as weightless as air. No earth, no sky, no colours other than a whiteness as thick as soap lather. When I closed my eyes, the clouds turned red, then black, and the white wings of the plane leaped like flames. On the yellow sand far below, a child lay on its face, red spittle flowing from the corner of its mouth. I could not see its face, but the fingers were stained with blue ink and small toes stuck out from a new green sandal. I shouted for my son, and I heard his voice, the same hoarseness and intermittent laugh like a gulp. I spun round, but it wasn't my son, it was a chubby, rosy-faced child talking in English.
– What's that land down there, Mummy?
– It's Egypt.
– What does Egypt mean, Mummy?
– I don't know. It's a country in north Africa.
Points of light in the distant black abyss quivered and resisted the night. One of those points was the lamp beside my bed, my bookshelf, my papers, my sorrows and my joys, the small pillow with some hairs of his head on it and drops of his sweat. His black eyes glistened with tears, his voice called to me and two little hands clutched mine, holding them like a chain. The English child was still laughing and playing. He was almost the same age, four and a half years old.
Through the microphone, a voice announced we were landing at Teheran Airport. The doors opened and people filed towards the exit of the airport. In front of the passport officer, I stood in my place in the long queue. Beside me was an Indian doctor I'd met who also did not have an entry visa. One of the airport officials took us to a side room and we showed him the conference papers with our names written in the members list. We pointed to the sentence which said that an entry visa could be given to any conference member who did not have the time to get one in their own country.
The room was crammed with people. A slender young

Iranian sat behind a small desk, his face pale and exhausted, drops of sweat on his forehead. On his desk was a pile of papers and passports. He looked up and glanced briefly at the Indian doctor, then at the picture in his passport. He raised his hand like a hammer over one of the empty pages and stamped in an entry visa. With the same speed, he looked at my photo in the passport, his eyes steady as he looked into my face, raised his hand and printed an entry visa on an empty page in my passport.

I found myself in the heart of Teheran, walking in Pahlavi Street, the same street along which I'd used to walk four times a day. Were it not for the iron partition dividing the street and the new buildings that stood in previously empty squares, I would not have believed it had been two years since I was there. The faces were almost the same, the men with their sharp features that contained the strength and courage of mountains, the women with their large black eyes and their short skirts. The cinema was still showing cowboy films, the nut and sweet seller with his golden teeth and black moustache still sat on the pavement, the pale sad boy with his small scales, the same old beggar still in her place crouched up against the wall, her empty hand stretched out in front of her.

Countries, like people, all have their own particular smell. That of Teheran was attractive in that it had in it the smell of the mountains and their melted snow that fell from the icy peaks in little streams, breaking over the rocks then running pure through the tall trees beside the curving-downward road.

I walked up the mountain towards Shamiran, to the narrow road, and stood before the small house. I still remembered the shape of the garden which I'd seen two years previously, the staircase leading to the reception room. As the door opened, I thought that the thin, tall, white-haired young man would appear as he had done in November 1968. But he did not. Instead, a young women swathed in black stood before me. I recognised her even though she was so pale and thin. It was Simin Danshwar, history of literature professor at Teheran University.

Dr Danshwar told me the story of the death of her husband, Jalal Al Ahmed. He had been spending his last summer holiday beside the sea at Qazwin, and she was with him, reading some verses of poetry to him after he had exercised on the beach. He had put his head down on a pillow and became silent forever. It was nighttime and the place was far from the town, with no electricity. She sought the help of some coastal workers. When they found out it was Jalal Al Ahmed, they came from all the huts, filled the lamps with gas and surrounded him with flowers. The carpenters worked till dawn making a decorated bier. Dr Danshwar's eyes filled with tears as she said:

– Jalal died amongst people who loved him, about whom he wrote. He died on 17 September 1969, nine months ago, aged forty-six. One year has not yet passed since he died. He died young.

– Was he ill? I asked her.

She looked around her, then whispered: I don't know.

We were sitting in a room looking out onto the garden. Silence descended suddenly. The rustle of the trees seemed like stealthy footsteps. A shiver ran through my body.

– Do you think the house is being watched? I whispered.

– I don't know, she said sadly.

At night, I left her alone in the small house in the mountains. She saw me to the garden gate, and stood before me holding the door. Before leaving the narrow street, I turned around to see her still standing in the soft light, still holding the door.

From the open window of my hotel room, I could see the high rise on top of which were the lights of the Hilton Hotel, beside it the Iranian Centre for International Conferences. Arranged in the large garden were tables, trays of food, glasses of wine and champagne and eight hundred people from all over the world. From Egypt, there was Doctor Surour and three other doctors, including myself.

In one of the seats reserved for the American delegation sat a doctor who announced that New York had issued a decision that year to legalise abortions. A voice from the Tunisian delegation declared that abortion was permitted in Tunisia. An English woman doctor spoke about the new understanding of sex. The American doctor spoke again and said that American society still blushed at hearing the word sex. A doctor from Sweden spoke of a new injection for women which prevented

conception for a whole year. A member of the Turkish delegation opposed the suppression of woman's body alone in the
matter of birth-control. The doctor from India spoke of sterilisation operations for men which are easy and external whereas
sterilisation for a woman entails a difficult operation.

I sat in silence through the conference, then raised a hand in
the final session and threw the question into the hall:

– Why do you want to control the birthrate?

Astonished, inquiring, staring eyes turned towards me. I had
no jewels around my neck, so they realised I was from a poor
Third World country. I did not have my name and title on my
chest, so they realised I had no name or title. A doctor objected
to the question and said that it had no relationship to the subject
of the conference, because the subject was the *means* of birth-
control. A Sudanese doctor objected to the objection and said
that the question was at the heart of the matter and it was not
possible to separate causes from symptoms. A doctor from the
Philippines interjected and said that the causes entered into the
sphere of social and not medical sciences.

The doctor from India said that there was no distinction nowadays between medicine and society. The Filipino doctor stood
up to answer, but the chairman banged on the table and called
for order. He gave the floor to an African doctor from Ghana
who was the first to raise his hand and gave a lecture on the
benefits of birth-control, especially in backward countries of
Africa, Asia and Latin America. The doctor from India objected to the word 'backward' and wanted to substitute the
word 'developing'. Dr Surour raised his hand and asked to
speak, explaining that backwardness was not a disgrace and
neither was poverty. The disgrace was in over-breeding like
rabbits. The Sudanese doctor objected to the word 'rabbits' and
said that poverty, not children, was the problem which had to
be dealt with first. The Swedish doctor asked about the reasons
for poverty in backward countries. The doctor from Sudan replied: imperialism. Here, the doctor from Kenya stood up and
said: This is a medical conference and has nothing to do with
politics. He proposed returning to the original topic of the conference. The chairman agreed to what the Kenyan doctor said
and the previous discussion was resumed. They began to talk

about types of uterine coils, the proportion of hormones in the new birth-control pills produced by an American company, large quantities of which it had sent to backward countries as development projects or military and economic aid.

I crept out by the back door into the street. The sun was about to set, lights reflected off the streams descending from the mountains. Around Shtanouja lay long and slender cars, stretching as far as the lawn beside the flowerbeds. In each car, a chauffeur sat at the ready by the steering wheel.

Behind one car stood a thin child, a yellow cloth in hand, who approached apprehensively to wipe the windows. The driver put his hand out of the window and waved him away as one would wave away a fly. A number of children came up to the driver, their eyes wide and bulging, the whites yellow, in the hand of each child a yellow cloth, the other hand open and stretched out, waiting for coins to fall from the sky.

I walked along the street leading down to town, crossing Pahlavi Street, which they call *Khayayan Pahlavi*. Queues of young people stood in front of the cinema showing a cowboy film, a naked woman in a seductive posture, men on horses carrying guns. There were other posters on the walls: a picture of the Shah and the Empress, advertisements for Kent cigarettes, Johnny Walker whisky, huge bottles of Coca Cola occupying spaces on the walls surrounded by revolving red, blue and yellow lights that flicked on and off.

I went into a small restaurant from which wafted the smell of shilo kebab – large Iranian bread, onions and red turnip. A group of young men sat at a table, a girl with them, her hair short and black.

– Haven't we met here before?
– Yes, two years ago.
– Your name is Mani.
– Yes.

I asked her who was writing in Iran now Jalal Al Ahmed was dead. She mentioned the name Abbas Bahlawan and said that Jalal al-Ahmed had created a bridge between Marxism and Islam. Abbas Bahlawan walked on this bridge, but he rejected dervishes and dervishism. His lastest book was called *No Dervish*.

*

The last night in Teheran I spent in Mani's room in a small alleyway. She lived alone in Teheran as her family was in a village near Shiraz. In the morning she went to university and in the evening worked with a group of fighters. She made me a glass of tea and sat down before me. She spoke and I listened:

– I have a friend in prison named Houma. She was stopped by SAVAK men whilst walking in the street. She was not carrying any leaflets. They put her in prison and began interrogating her. They removed her brassière and then one of the officers began to burn her nipples with a lit cigarette. The pain almost killed her and she started to confess everything. That night, the police raided some houses and arrested a number of our student colleagues. The men of SAVAK and the CIA have made a film on the art of interrogating revolutionaries, particularly women and girls. America has distributed thousands of copies of this film as part of 'cultural aid' to friendly countries such as Taiwan, the Philippines and Indonesia. We no longer meet in houses or public places, but in mosques, the only places into which SAVAK or the CIA cannot go.

The Shah is semi-isolated and America directs him in everything; they try to present him as the 'father' of the Iranian people, in accordance with popular tradition. Every week he goes to pray in one of the mosques, trying to wrench leadership away from the Imams and the Ayatollahs. The people are foiled into thinking that he is a good, god-fearing man, but he is corrupt in both his private and public life. He takes the wealth of the people and his many love affairs are public knowledge, even to his wife Farah Dibba whom he regards as a mere means to an heir. He respects neither her, nor women in general. His idea of establishing a ministry for women's affairs is only an attempt to win the support of women in return for giving them some superficial rights.

Mani's voice stayed in my ears during the flight back to Cairo.
The years passed and I forgot her words, or so it seemed. Until the Iranian Revolution in 1978. Then her voice, her large black eyes as she sat in front of me in her white dress, came back to me. The Shah was thrown out of Iran and could find

no country to accept him. Even his American friends abandoned him.

I believed that the Iranian Revolution would liberate the Iranian people, that the hopes of Mani and her colleagues would be realised. But it was soon aborted by Khomeini and his aides and changed from a revolution of liberation to another force of tyranny in the name of religion.

In November 1984, in London, I met a professor who had been forced to flee from the tyranny of Khomeini and his aides and was living in exile with some members of his family who had fled with him. He had a small daughter who had not managed to escape with them and who was in prison in Iran. His wife did not sleep at night in London, thinking about her daughter imprisoned in Teheran and about other Iranian women and girls upon whom Khomeini's government had imposed the *chador* of grey, black, brown, dark blue or green. Anyone not wearing one of these colours was punished by dismissal from her job or imprisonment. Many women and girls had been imprisoned or executed. Those young men who were not in prison or who had not been executed had been enlisted by Khomeini into the war against Iraq. Around the neck of each young man hung a metal key with which to open the gate of heaven after dying in the war.

The professor's wife spoke without tears, but her eyes were filled with sadness. And something other than sadness: anger, determination and challenge. I was reminded of the eyes of Dr Simin Danshwar and also of her husband, Jalal Al Ahmed.

At the door of their small house, the professor and his wife saw me off, as Jalal Al Ahmed and Danshwar had done. As I walked to the street, I said to myself:

– There will be another revolution in Iran.

On the walls of the underground station I read the words *Down with Khomeini* written in black, in Farsi. I remembered the same letters from years ago, but instead of the word 'Khomeini' had been the words 'the Shah'.

PART SEVEN

India

My journey to India was unlike any other journey to any other country. It was the journey of a whole life, from birth to death, like a circle beginning and ending at the same point; but not the same point, because birth is not death and the beginning is not the end.

Those who love travelling may wonder why I feel like this about India in particular, when there are many countries and places in the world to dazzle the tourist. But for me, tourism is not flying in planes, visiting museums, sleeping and eating in luxury hotels. Tourism for me means walking around the streets and dusty quarters, discovering people everywhere, especially in those places from which tourists run or where they put their handkerchiefs to their noses should they happen to pass by.

My journey to India was long and exhausting. But it was enjoyable, like a journey to the self with all its hardship and sweetness. It was perhaps the most difficult journey of my life even though I have visited most countries of the world and have trodden the roughest of paths. The difficulty of discovering India was very much like the difficulty of discovering oneself; for although the self is part of one, how much time and effort it takes to know one's self. India is like this too. In as much as you know your self, you know her. In as much as you have your self, India gives of her self. Perhaps this is the reason that some people see only dust and poverty in India and others can penetrate the surface and reach to its heart.

Before the plane landed in New Delhi Airport, the stewardess announced it was seven in the morning. I looked at my watch and realised that in Cairo people were still asleep (the sun rises in India three and a half hours earlier than in Egypt). It was

January and I was wearing a woollen coat, but as soon as I landed in India I took it off. The winter sun in India was warm and soft and sent a sort of pleasure and optimism through my body.

I waited for the luggage to arrive with a large crowd of tourists and travellers, most of them foreigners with white skins tinged red, their clothes luxurious, their cases large and expensive, some of them (tourists) with cameras hanging from their shoulders, others (experts, of course) holding Samsonite cases. I come across such people in every airport, I know the movements they make, the air of superiority in their blue eyes when they look at brown faces such as mine or at Indian faces, grumbling at the sight of old suitcases and worn clothes, as though travelling by plane were their sole right as though the money with which they bought their expensive clothes and large suitcases were not originally the wealth of brown toiling faces, the rightful owners of the land and of the country.

The Indian faces around me reminded me of faces in my country – the same humble smile that at times resembles the smile of those who feel weak or embarrassed or meek. That smile is one of the legacies of colonialism and how I prefer lines of anger. An Indian gives up his seat humbly to an arrogant European. The European goes and takes his place without so much as a thank you or smile for the Indian. I hold back my anger and throw the European a look of hatred and contempt.

I carried my case by myself, although a number of porters surrounded me, each one wanting to carry it for me. I was reminded of Cairo Airport and felt sad: I never saw such sights in European or American airports, but poverty in India or Egypt or in Asian and African countries is only one legacy those people – colonialists from Europe and America – left behind. Tourists forget this fact and grumble at the sight of porters competing to carry cases or when they are greeted by the sight of beggars. And how the tourist in India complains about the number of beggars!

Through my travelling experience I have found that first impressions are the most important ones, the most truthful. I got into the habit of recording my first impressions of any new country to which I travelled, before it grew familiar to my eyes and before this familiarity weakened the eyes' sensitivity to new things and the new became so familiar the eyes hardly saw them.

And I don't mean the eyes or seeing alone, but feelings too. From the moment I landed on Indian soil, I felt deep feelings of ease, peace and calm engulf me. I do not know why. Was it the humble, submissive smile of the people? Or the clear blue sky and the sun? Or that old man sitting on the pavement looking at people and life with a tenderness and detachment? Or was it those birds singing everywhere, landing everywhere, snatching food from the midst of a group of people? Or those cows grazing in the streets beside cars and motorcycles and bicycles, eating everywhere without anyone objecting?

I told myself that if these birds and cows were safe in India, then that was why I too felt safe and secure. Later I learned that Indians respect life in all forms, that Indian philosophy is based on the sanctity of life and on not killing any living being, not even a mosquito. One Indian sect, named the 'Jinia', calls on its devotees to wear nose-masks and to walk lightly and bare-foot so as to protect innocent ants and insects from being crushed. The mask is to protect small innocent gnats and mosquitoes from entering the nose of the devotee and dying.

I was very surprised by the Indians' regard and respect for life, and I could not help laughing at those barefoot, masked men whom I sometimes met in the street. With their white clothes and masks I took them for doctors who had come out of operating theatres looking for an escaped patient, or for people with some nose disease or an obsession with germs or who had come from a mental hospital. When I learned that they were devotees of the 'Jinia' sect and that they covered their noses, not to protect themselves from germs but to protect germs from themselves, I realised how a great principle can sometimes be turned into a sort of madness, how religions can sometimes contain contradictions, exaggerations and nonsense.

It is difficult to know a country just from its capital. In most cases, capitals of countries are big cities that resemble each other, with embassies, government offices, wide clean streets that get larger and cleaner as you approach the governors' houses or offices or the places where their deputies or representatives or suchlike work. The capital of New Delhi is no different from any other capital in this respect. I was amazed at some of the luxurious modern houses set in lush gardens and those beautiful wide streets which lead you to the upper-class quarters where wealthy Indians, foreigners and tourists live.

But as soon as you enter Old Delhi, as they call it, the streets narrow and are crowded with bodies and souls. You can hardly tell the pavement from the road, can hardly make out all the vehicles that move around. There are vehicles that you know are cars or motorcycles or bicycles and some that are almost a combination of all three. In India you can see transport that dates from the time the wheel was invented; starting with the elephant or camel or bullock or boar, all kinds of animals here pull any cart along any street, and all forms of transport, from the wheel moved by human feet to the wheel moved by motor to the motorcycle, then to the car, all running and racing through the same street. And walking through the streets, you can also see the classes: those who ride in cars are the ruling class – wealthy Indians and foreigners and those with comfortable professions; those who ride motorcycles are petty businessmen and civil servants; those riding bicycles are of the poor and working classes. The lowest class in India are those who do not ride anything but who pull the wheels (like bullocks and donkeys). One of the most familiar sights in India is that thin emaciated man panting, face and body dripping with sweat, pulling three or four people on his cart.

But this thin panting man is better off than many others, for he still has the power to pull something. There are those who have lost this power and are only able to lie on the pavement awaiting the final moment. On the pavement everywhere in India you see men and women and children whose only shelter is the bit of pavement on which they lie.

Some tourists in India see this poverty as romantic; some of them stop in pained shock without realising the real reason for this poverty. Still others accuse the poor of laziness or stupidity; some say that this is the will of God, that God bestows a livelihood on those He wants and denies it to others; some believe that poverty is an Indian philosophy and a kind of desire to abstain from the enjoyment of life. The tourist is capable of thinking anything other than the real reason. What one tourist spends in one day is sufficient to feed an Indian family for one month. But the enormous wealth of India does not go to the rightful owners of the land but into the pockets of foreign invaders, foreign companies.

I do not know why I recalled my childhood when I was in India. It was no ordinary recollection of incidents but rather strong and oppressive feelings that came over me as I looked into the faces of Indian children, for I would suddenly feel that this child standing before me was myself as a child, that this look in his eyes was exactly the same as mine when a child, that the way in which he showed off or ran or played or carried his small brother was my way as a child.

One of the most common sights in India is of children playing, carrying their young brothers or sisters in a particular way, the little one sitting on the bigger child's hip, legs dangling. These are lucky children who come out of their houses to play in the streets or gardens, for most children know of nothing called play but instead work and scratch around for a livelihood in the fields or factories or small shops. There are also children who stand in your way in the streets with their thin hands held out, saying in English, give me *bakshish*. An unforgettable sight is those children who do not stand in your way and who do not say anything, but who look at you with silent eyes that contain only one persistent and clear meaning, shouted without sound: We are hungry!

Strange feelings were constantly with me in India every time I saw a child or went into a house or temple or office or school or hospital or factory. Strange feelings, as though I were not in India but in Egypt. Despite superficial differences there was a sort of strange resemblance, as though the roots were the same. Discovering India was like discovering Egypt. I began to understand the history of Egypt from the history of India, to see things about Egypt that I had not seen when I was in Egypt. This is not just because a person only learns about his country when he's outside it or only sees a thing clearly from a distance, but because the general features of India resembled the general features of Egypt. Even the smell of the air and dust were almost the same as the smell of the air and dust of Egypt.

Everywhere I went, people would ask: Have you seen the Taj Mahal? When I said no, eyes would widen in surprise and I'd hear them say: Then you haven't seen India. It reminded me of the pyramids in Egypt. Many people imagine that the most important things in Egypt are the pyramids, just as many think that what's most important in India is the Taj Mahal. In my opinion, this is not true. I am not one of those who worship ancient monuments and buildings. Whenever I see a huge monument or a magnificent building, the question always comes to my mind: Who built it and why? However beautiful a building may be, I only see its beauty after knowing the story behind it. How many reprehensible stories there are behind the most beautiful monuments and buildings. How many pyramids have been built with the blood and sweat of thousands of hungry slaves.

The most beautiful lampshades in the world were made with the skin of men and women murdered by Hitler in Nazi prisons. The Taj Mahal, the most beautiful building in the world, was built by the hands of thousands of hungry Indians over twenty years. They say that the Mogul emperor cut off the arms of the engineer who built it so that he could never build one like it for any other emperor. And yet the Taj Mahal has come to symbolise love: on moonlit nights, you can see parties of lovers and tourists looking at this white marble building, marvelling at this Mogul emperor who built it for his beloved wife after she died. The Taj Mahal is simply the tomb of a wife of a Mogul ruler, but it was built in expensive marble topped by splendid marble domes, on its inner and outer walls marvellous multi-coloured engravings.

I saw the Taj Mahal at Agra, as people advised me to, by the light of the sun *and* of the moon. With my fingers I touched the marble walls as smooth as the skin of the wives of emperors and kings, and I went down the stairs inside to see the sarcophagus embedded with marble mosaics and precious stones under which the wife was buried. I was told that the money spent on building the Taj Mahal would have been enough to build up India and make her a most advanced country.

Surely we need to revise the meaning of history, for history is not only the life or death of kings and rulers; neither is history simply buildings – fortresses and pyramids. History is more than that: history is the story of millions of people and their continuous struggle for survival. History is the resistance of these millions in the face of their rulers. The ruler who deserves to be remembered by history is the one who tried to provide the millions in his country with a decent life, not the one who ridiculed the millions and enslaved them in order to build an expensive marble tomb for the body of his wife who had done nothing in her life other than eat and sleep.

The Taj Mahal, in my opinion, does not symbolise the love between an emperor and his wife, but rather a love that was lost in history and buried beneath a tomb of white marble.

In the capital of India, New Delhi, I stayed with my husband who had been working in India for two years, in his small and simple apartment. I realised for the first time that it was preferable for a wife to be a guest in her husband's house. She always feels happy, because her stay is only temporary, not permanent. I learned too that distance renews love and affection. I always knew this fact and said that a happy couple live in two separate rooms, leaving a space between them. As this thought developed, I said that a happy couple live in two separate apartments. But now, after my thinking has matured, I say that a happy couple live in two separate countries, that distance weakens fragile marital relations but strengthens firm ones based on feelings of true love, mutual respect and understanding.

Narayan was the name of the Indian boy who cooked my husband's food. He was a brown, small and thin boy who walked with a strange lightness, as though he were concerned about stepping too heavily on the earth. I noticed that many Indians walk this way. Later I found out that it is a kind of humility that characterises the Indians; a sort of delicateness and desire to respect living beings, even if they are small insects runnning across the ground.

I learned from Narayan that his only task in life was cooking.

He would not, for example, wash the car or sweep the house, even if it meant double the wages. This was not because he did not need such wages, but because such jobs were assigned to a certain caste whereas he was from a higher caste. He only washed men's clothes, so that while he could wash my husband's clothes, he refused to do mine.

Indian society still makes a strong distinction between castes. The highest caste is the Brahmin caste, the lowest the caste of servants known as the Untouchables or the Pariahs. These are people whose touch people shun because they are poor and unclean. Some Indian leaders like Gandhi and Nehru tried to combat this caste discrimination, and it has indeed lessened, but it has not completely disappeared.

Members of the untouchable caste must not go near members of other castes and can only speak with them from a certain distance so that their breath does not reach the noses of the others. I was told that some wealthy Brahmins would take a bath if the shadow of an Untouchable fell on them.

Every day I would wake up in the early morning to the sound of a terrible siren, like an air-raid warning. I discovered it really was an air-raid siren, but it was used in times of peace like a public bell to tell people it was the start of the day. It is not a bad idea for those who work, but it can be annoying for someone who is not used to it or who like myself stays up at night and wants to rest late into the day.

But people in Delhi did not stay up like people in Cairo. Most of them went to sleep before ten at night and woke up very early. If you walked in the streets at six in the morning, you would find crowds and carts and motorcycles and hear the radio playing Indian songs in the shops and houses.

But you only saw cars in the streets after nine. Work in government offices started at ten in the morning and ended at six in the evening. The English system still exists in India. The English used to get up early and go to the club to play golf before it got too hot. Then they'd take a shower and by the time they got to their offices it was already ten o'clock. Most Indian civil servants neither went to the club in the morning nor played golf, but they woke up at six and sat in their houses drinking tea and chatting until nearly ten. Some of them told me that this English system did not suit the hot Indian climate and that it would be better to start work at six before it got hot and to utilise those lost morning hours.

Indians would come into your house at any time. You might, for example, be lying in bed and be caught unawares by your Indian neighbour entering your bedroom. They also left the doors of their houses open so that you could go in at any time. They reminded me of the people of my village, Kufr Tahla. How I loved such simple customs which broke down the artificial barriers between people. But it could also be frustrating, especially at those times when one wanted to be alone or completely isolated from others. Indians in general did not isolate themselves from each other, except if they practiced yoga or were Buddhist or Hindu monks who spent their lives in total isolation meditating on the eternal, absolute self.

I was in bed reading an Indian novel. It was one o'clock in the morning when I heard a strange banging noise in the street. I opened the shutters and saw an Indian man walking slowly, in his hand a large stick with which he struck the street at every step. I thought he was the *mas'harati* who walked around the streets in Egypt during the fast of Ramadan waking people up to take their last meal before daybreak. I asked my husband:
– Is he the *mas'harati*? Do Indians fast during Ramadan too?
– He's not a *mas'harati*, my husband laughed. He's the night watchman of this area.
– Why does he bang on the ground so loudly? I asked.
– So that the people in the houses will know he's awake and vigilant.
– But, I said, with this noise he also tells thieves which street he's guarding, so they can rush off to another street to rob people, certain the watchman isn't there.
– That's exactly what happens, my husband chuckled. The watchman's stick only awakens the sleeping and alerts the thieves to where he is.
At the beginning of the month, the watchman would come to our apartment and ask for his monthly wage. There was

another reason for the stick he banged at night. He was telling people: I do my duty every night and so deserve the wages you pay.

Poverty in India drives many people to invent strange occupations in order to get some sort of wage. A common sight in New Delhi was those ironing men whom you saw pulling a wooden handcart to a stop in front of a house. The servant would come out with a basket of clothing and the ironing man would work rapidly until he finished, then drag his cart off to another house and so on. When you walked in the streets in the morning, you would find these ironing men standing in front of the houses ironing clothes on their small wooden carts.

At any time of day, the door bell would ring and you'd find an Indian man offering you his services unsolicited. He might tell you he was prepared to buy new furniture for your house, if you were an old resident of the quarter. If you were a new resident, he would offer to furnish your apartment, or even find you another apartment.

Once a tinsmith rang the doorbell. Whilst he was there, I discovered that one of the taps needed a new washer to stop the water dripping. The man took out his many tools (they looked like a surgeon's) and began a long examination of the tap. Finally he said it was no longer any good, a new one had to be fitted. He reminded me of tinsmiths in Egypt who, when you ask them to fit a new washer in a tap, tell you that you should fit a new tap and then, of course, ask an exorbitant price. Remembering this, I said to the Indian tinsmith:

– No, I know this method from Egypt.

The Indian laughed because I had seen through his stratagem, and fitted a washer for a reasonable price.

I loved wandering around the popular quarters, looking at the small shops and the crowds, listening to the sounds and smelling the strong odours everywhere. But I preferred living in a quiet area far from the noise and the bustle. Even in my husband's quarter, the quiet was not complete. As soon as the sun rose in the early morning, the birds left their nests in the trees in enormous numbers and began singing loudly. In Egypt, whenever I heard birds singing, my heart would rejoice at the sweet and gentle sound. But when this sweet and gentle sound is multiplied hundreds of times, it loses its gentleness and sweetness and becomes more like a screech. The birds in India were numerous and bold, sometimes so bold that they would swoop over your head and pluck the bread from out of your hand. They were as bold as the cows that grazed in the streets.

The clamour of the birds would give way to the clamour of itinerant sellers going from house to house carrying on their heads or on their carts different types of vegetables or fruit or any other commodity. The clamour of the sellers would give way to a man with a monkey or snake doing the rounds with someone singing Indian songs or blowing on wooden pipes. The monkey would dance to the tunes and the snake would begin its acrobatics. People watched from their balconies and threw down money. Sometimes the singer was not one man but a whole troupe of singers with pipes and tambourines, and the movements of the monkey or snake would be accompanied by an elephant ridden by the leader or a magician who slept on nails, ate fire or flew through the air on a magic carpet.

I found I did not always need to leave the house to learn about India – because India comes to your very door. But India has more than one face. How many different faces India has!

We were in the month of January. The weather in New Delhi was like spring in Egypt. The sun was warm and gentle, the breeze refreshing, neither hot nor cold, its touch hardly tangible, as though it were body temperature. In Delhi Airport, we waited for the plane to take us to the south of India, to the region of tea plantations. My husband read the *Indian Times* whilst I watched the people in the airport. Airports are like capital cities, international places where all nationalities, colours and languages mix – in other words, places without nationality or colour or language. For this reason they are attractive and repulsive at the same time. Faces (including my own) melt into one featureless face.

But Delhi Airport does have a definite personality, I don't know why. Perhaps because of the Indian women wearing saris and red spots in the centre of their foreheads. In the centre of each glass airport door there was also a red spot.

The Indian plane flew through the vast, ever-stretching sky. India is thirty-six times larger than Egypt and it takes hours to fly from place to place.

The plane landed at Madras in southern India. From the intense heat and the humidity I knew that I was on the equator and directly under the sun's rays. I took off some clothing, the sweat beginning to pour from my face. The faces in southern India were dark brown, like those of people in equatorial Africa, except that the shape of faces here were more delicate, the nose upturned and pointed, the lips thin, the black hair soft and not frizzy, the eyes shining in attractive brown faces.

We walked on the Madras coast, part of the Indian Ocean. The sea breeze only succeeded in lowering the temperature a little. I have never grown used to intense heat that is very humid, and in equatorial regions I feel I'm choking. The earth seems to me to have become part of hell, without a breath of air.

I hurried towards the bus that would take us to the tea plantations in the mountains. My breathing quietened a little and the sweat dried as we began to climb. The air became fresher and carried the smell of equatorial trees and flowers of all kinds and colours. The small Indian bus followed the spiral mountain road and at every bend the brown Indian driver would press the horn. The road was very narrow and it would have been easy for the bus to collide with one of the tea-carrying lorries coming down the mountain.

I noticed that most of these lorries bore the name 'Tata'. When I inquired who Tata was, I learned he was an Indian millionaire who owned lorries, hotels, a number of companies, and industrial and commercial projects in India. Everywhere in India you see the name Tata on everything. The enormous wealth of India still goes into the pockets of a small handful of people, some Indian, some English. Despite being independent, India is still part of the Commonwealth, and landowners and money owners still support a feudal capitalist system and vigorously oppose any socialist tendency.

The air grew cooler and dryer as we climbed the mountain. Dense trees which had covered the mountains gave way to a green carpet of smaller tea shrubs that stretched to the horizon.

The tea plant is very strange, with a particular disposition; it needs special conditions for growing and flowering; a certain soil and certain height, no less than four thousand feet above sea level, a certain temperature and amount of sun, rain and shade. The best type of tea grows at a height of 7,000 feet above sea level. Tall trees grew in orderly fashion between the tea shrubs. I thought they were wild but I learned that they were planted to shade the tea leaves from the intense heat of the sun.

The tea plant lives a hundred years, during which it produces a large amount of tea leaves. The brown Indian women come every morning carrying large baskets on their backs and with their fast experienced fingers pick the soft upper leaves. The planting, harvesting and production of tea in India is largely women's work. Whoever follows tea from its planting in the fields until it becomes a glass of tea knows that behind the pleassure in this glass are thousands of people, most of them women, who work from sunrise to sunset for a few Indian rupees that provide a bare existence.

Before a girl is ten years old she goes with her mother to the field to work in the tea plantations or to the factory to participate in the tea production. In some villages boys and men also work, but there are regions where only women and girls work. Men are a higher, leisured sex that sit in front of the houses all day long, smoking and drinking and playing backgammon or tricktrack.

Early one morning I sat in a small car beside an Indian translator. I had asked to speak to those women who worked to provide for their children and husbands. The women spoke a local Indian language and I had to take a local translator who knew English.

The morning started bright, but grey clouds soon gathered over the mountain peaks and it began to pour. When it rains in these mountainous equatorial regions, the sky turns into an ocean that empties its waters onto the mountains without clemency or respite.

– What's your name? I asked the young Indian translator.
– My name's Bujan, he said.
– And your father's name?

– I don't carry my father's name, but my mother's; her name is Pravati after the goddess Pravati, wife of the god Shiva.

– Does everyone here carry their mother's names? I asked.

– No. Most people here have neither their mother's nor their father's names. They carry only their own names. The father's name is only one letter.

The driver broke in and said:

– My name is M Narayan. The 'M' is the first letter of my father's name, but my own principal name is Narayan. This is the reverse of what the English do, since their principal name is the last one which is the father's or grandfather's, whereas the personal name is only the first letter.

– Which do you prefer? I asked him.

– Of course, that my last and principal name should be my own name and not that of my father or mother or grandfather.

I laughed and asked him:

– Don't you want your children to be named after you?

– No, he said vehemently. Each of my sons and daughters should have their own name.

The young translator interrupted:

– Many of the men here don't worry about lineage like they do in the north, for example, because women here often marry more than one man. Sometimes five or six or seven brothers marry one women. Lineage from the father is not important here and men don't think about it much.

– Do women enjoy a high status here? I asked.

– Yes, he said. In some regions the woman works and provides for her children and husbands, except if she's dominated by the man and he takes her wages, as happens in some tea plantation areas.

The car drew up in front of a pretty little house built on a hillside and surrounded on all sides by a beautiful garden full of perfumed equatorial flowers and mango and guava trees particular to the region. An Indian man, the overseer of this plantation, welcomed us. The plantation, owned by an Indian company, covered an area of 900 feddan and was ranged in green terraces from the bottom to the top of the mountain. Nine hundred and ten men and women worked on it, the majority women. I asked to go and talk to the women but the manager said that the climb was difficult because the mountain was steep.

– How do the women workers go up? I asked him.

– They're used to it, he replied.

– I'm a woman and I'm ready and able to climb, I said.

The young translator accompanied me and we climbed through the rows of tea shrubs. After a few minutes I began panting and the young Indian smiled and said:

– Each of these women go up and down this difficult path many times a day carrying a large basket of tea leaves on her back. At dusk she comes down with her basket to the door of the factory where she empties her load and gets her wages according to the amount she has gathered.

We reached one of the rows of women. They stood at regular intervals in the rows of tea shrubs, on the back of each a huge basket, fingers plucking the highest tea leaves very quickly and exactly. They looked at me in surprise and stared at my clothes and face. Then they began to laugh and talk in a Tamil language I did not understand.

I chose one with bright and vivacious eyes from amongst the thin brown faces and asked her:

– What's your name?

– Sarouja.

– How old are you?

– Seventeen.

– Are you married? I asked.

– Yes.

I noticed that some of the women wore whole saris while others had only half saris. I learned that it is the married women who wear whole saris. They marry very young, work the whole day, and when they go home at the end of the day they cook the food, clean the house and do the washing.

– Have you been to school? I asked Sarouja.

– We don't go to school, she answered.

– What does your husband do?

– He works with me on the plantation.

– Do you have any children?

– Two, she said.

– But you're still young. How many children will you have by the time you're thirty?

– I'll only have these two, because my husband went to the doctor and was sterilised.

I learned from the plantation manager that the health supervisors on the plantation advised the men and women workers to limit their children to two or three so that the mother should not be distracted from plantation work by her children. On the plantation there was a home where children were raised for work in the field or the factory. This was a whole settlement of men, women and children whose lives were organised to the last detail to serve one purpose – the production of tea. The profits made on this tea did not return to them but to the plantation and factory owners.

In the tea factory I saw thin brown faces behind the machines working without stop. I saw the thin pale bodies of children looking towards the tea-covered mountains, realising that their future was, like that of their mothers and fathers, in the field or the factory. In the houses of the workers I saw that they slept on old mats on the floor. When I went into the manager's elegant house, he offered me a glass of quality tea on a silver tray. When the manager noticed that I had difficulty swallowing it, he asked me:

– Don't you like the tea? It's first grade.

– Is there first and second grade tea? I asked.

– Yes, of course, he said. First grade tea is completely clean of chaff. It's not sold in the market but is sent by special order to kings and emperors and heads of state.

– And second grade tea? I asked.

– It is mixed with other kinds of tea and some chaff remains in it. Third grade tea is not cleaned at all.

– Is there a fourth grade? I asked.

– Yes, he said. It's called tea dust and is what remains after the tea is sieved. This is the tea that's sold in local Indian markets.

– This is what those who grow and produce the tea drink? I said, distressed.

– Yes, he replied without understanding the reason for my question.

And so I learned that these women and men who work all day long on the tea plantations and in their factories do not even taste the tea which they plant and produce with their own hands, sweat and blood.

The streets of the large cities in India, like Delhi and Bombay and Calcutta, all resemble each other. In almost every street you see a huge number of people riding bicycles or motorbikes, or half motorbikes, half bicycles, half cars. Sometimes a whole family – father, mother and children – ride on one cycle or motorbike: a useful and practical way of beating the transportation problem. Women ride bikes despite their long saris which fly out in the wind and get caught in the spokes. A strange contradiction still surrounds the working Indian woman. She has broken down the barriers and has tackled everything, except discarding the sari which any Indian woman agrees is an impractical dress that hampers her steps and makes her stumble, not only on buses or bikes but even whilst walking. While some women say that the sari is feminine, others reply that femininity can go to hell; women should wear practical clothes, like trousers for example, to help them move easily and quickly. Some women say that the sari distinguishes Indian women from others in the world; others reply that what should distinguish Indian women from other women is the way they think and not the way they dress. The argument grows furious: some Indian men intervene to say that they prefer the sari; women rebel and say that a woman should wear the clothes in which she is comfortable and which let her move and work easily, not the clothes that men prefer.

But in general women in India still want to please men. In most families it is the man who dominates; the male children get more care, better food and more education than female children.

It is the woman in India who pays the dowry to her husband. The dowry increases the higher his class, position and education. This is a throw-back to the matriarchal system which used to prevail in India. The woman dominated inside and outside the home. She was the one who worked and owned property and inherited and was the head of the family. The children descended from her. After woman lost her supremacy the system of dowry payment did not change, the woman still paid the dowry to her husband.

An Indian woman doctor called Rumatalla ('Compassion of Allah' in Arabic) told me:

– People were happy to have a daughter when the woman held supremacy and lineage, but now fathers and mothers rejoice for male children, not for female ones. A son is like a golden egg, whereas a daughter is the one who pays the dowry and pays with her life for the sake of husband and children, without getting anything.

It is strange that so many Indian men hold such backward ideas about women, as if they have forgotten their own history. One of them, an educated doctor, said:

– The woman was made to be a servant in the house. Her mental capacities equip her only for such work.

A woman answered him:

– But Indira Gandhi is a woman and her mental capacities have helped her to govern in India. Is she a man or a woman?

He was quiet for a moment, as though he had forgotten it was a woman who governed India, then said:

– Yes, she's a woman, but a woman's a woman.

– What do you mean *a woman's a woman?* she asked.

He tried to answer using such words as femininity and masculinity. I realised that, even if they are ruled by a woman, men's thinking and views on women, and especially wives, stay the same; the patriarchal marriage or family in which men grow up is the principal seat of such ideas, and with the continuation of patriarchal marriage these ideas will remain in the minds of men (and women too) whether they are governed by a man or a woman.

I read in an Indian morning paper that thousands of Indian Muslims in Madras in the south prayed with other Indians to the god of rain to take pity on the people and save them from the severe drought that had happened in the region. The newspaper said that rain had poured down 82 hours after the prayers. Many people believed that the god of rain had brought the rain, even though meteorologists said that the rains had fallen because clouds had gathered in the region and because of a fall in temperature due to winds from the ocean.

Some customs in India made me think of the Middle Ages, when people explained rain, storms and natural disasters in religious terms. Some people in India still believe in hocus-pocus.

A widow in India is sometimes treated as a witch was in the Middle Ages. Until relatively recently an Indian wife would burn herself after her husband died, or her family would tie her up and throw her onto her husband's funeral pyre (it is still Hindu custom to cremate the dead). This custom has died out in most regions of India, but the widow is still despised. Some people hold her responsible for her husband's death, some believe her to be the reason for the natural catastrophes that sometimes occur. I feel sad for those millions of Indians kneeling in their temples every morning before the god Shiva to ward off disease or drought or hunger, not realising that neither Shiva nor other gods can prevent hunger but that what *does* prevent it would be the fair distribution of India's wealth to its people rather than it being snatched up by a minority inside and imperialists outside.

Brahma, Vishnu, Shiva; these are the three principal gods of power, creation and destruction in India. They say that the god that is able to create is also able to destroy. Thus Shiva symbolises both creation and destruction. Statues of Shiva come in many forms, the most important of which is the one that dances and has four arms, blood dripping from one of them and a murdered child under his foot. The story is that the goddess Pravati, Shiva's wife, gave birth to a son, but Shiva, believing that she had been unfaithful and that the boy was not his, took a sword and beheaded the child.

The goddess Pravati was angered by this and gave her son the head of an elephant. He lived and became the god Janeesh with an elephant's head and a human body, symbolising love, goodness and fortune. Indians kneel before him for his blessing and feel love and affection towards him. As for the god Shiva, they are frightened of him and fear his evil and treachery, so they shower him with money and food to appease him. They do not know that the money and food does not go to Shiva but to a class of priests and devotees who have made the temples into institutions that pour goodness onto themselves.

Something else I read in the morning paper: the ruler of Maharashtra (the capital of which is Bombay), admitted in a speech when opening a large exhibition that when he was ambassador to France he wanted to steal one of the beautiful art objects from a museum in Paris. But he fought against this desire and did not steal it. This ruler went on to say: I must admit that this impulse to steal was the strongest impulse I've had in my life, even though I do sometimes have the tendency to steal other things that please me.

Such frankness is in keeping with the direct and simple nature of Indians. They sometimes express themselves with an honesty that surprises foreigners. Some people think that this honesty is a sort of foolishness or stupidity or naiveté. In Egypt, when people want to make fun of someone frank and naive, they call him an Indian. But I respected the honesty and frankness of the Indians. I respected the ruler of Maharashtra who admitted that he stole or was inclined to steal sometimes. Many rulers steal without admitting it.

Indians in general are also good at flattery. Flattery is a form of social lying, widespread throughout the world that has become a sign of progress and sophistication. Indians treat their ministers and rulers with simplicity, without that tremor that we always see in our official meetings. I attended a large meeting in Delhi and saw the minister arrive and leave without fuss and bother. It all seemed natural and familiar. Later I learned that Indians (even if they are civil servants) are used to frank discussion and criticism, fearless of the head of state. This is due to the multiplicity of parties in India, to the existence of opposition parties that criticise the government and encourage people to express their opinions without fear.

In New Delhi, the capital of India, there is a famous garden called Ludi. I walked along one of its stone paths between open green spaces and flower beds. My image was reflected off the clear lake and with the approach of sunset a purple lily on the surface of the water began to close its leaves like a child folding its arms around its body and sleeping alone in the open air. The setting sun was as warm as body temperature, colouring the clouds red and orange. It fell behind the walls of Mogul buildings and penetrated the holes in the small curved Islamic-style doors. A young man standing on top of a Mogul dome began singing in a beautiful voice full of sweetness and strength that echoed off the high walls and raised curved dome. I did not understand the words of the song but the voice, tune and face of the boy made me stop and listen. Some young people, children and an old man stopped walking and began to listen. The eyes of the children shone like pieces of agate, their large black pupils gleaming, but the whites of their eye tinged with yellow. Most eyes in India are tinged yellow, like the eyes of those suffering from jaundice or chronic liver disease.

An American tourist stopped to listen to the song. The children gathered around him, their faces supplicant, their arms outstretched and waiting, dejected by poverty and deprivation despite the intelligent shining look in their eyes.

The boy continued singing beneath the black Mogul dome, the sad, strong voice calling out to the sky. The sun had completely disappeared, leaving only a redness over the clouds and tree tops. A cool breeze blew and dark shadows fell across the old building with a head as black as that of the monster I used to imagine as a child listening to stories and fairy tales. The word Mogul reminded me of a history class when I was ten years old. The Moguls invaded India and ruled it for three centuries, from the fourth to the tenth. The remains of Mogul buildings still stood here, their abandoned black domes creating the impression that cruel-hearted invaders lived inside.

Indian faces are peaceful and quiet, but also somewhat submissive and dejected, like the faces of some people in Egypt. The Moguls and the English left their mark on the faces of the people in the countries they colonised, but here in India their marks are stronger. For six centuries they drained the country's wealth and the most important monument they left behind was poverty.

Hearing about poverty in India is not like seeing it. Poverty is a living death that fills the cities and streets with deformed ghosts. Mothers, like great skeletons, carry children who are nothing but eyes and bones. Bodies lie on the pavement covered with millions of flies as though they are a pile of garbage, veined arms outstretched, cupped hands waiting for someone to throw something to eat into the palm. It is a steady tableau of the human struggle for survival. Beggars everywhere, even in airports, hungry children, blind youngsters. Sufferers from lung tuberculosis, faces scarred by smallpox so numerous that you begin to consider them as an integral part of life.

Here hunger sweeps over life like a flood. It does not come, but is an ever present and permanent feature of life. People are transformed into protruding black eyes, neither alive nor dead, even though their hearts continue to beat in a way that even doctors do not understand.

In India I found life full of contradictions: whilst thousands of Indians were dying of hunger, vast quantities of food were donated to religious temples. One deals with these contradictions by separating one from the other as though there were no relationship between them. Belief in a religious idea may live side by side with scientific experience. Belief in celestial bodies and stars exists side by side with astronomy, devotion to worldly pleasures, drinking, sexual enjoyment alongside a philosophy of abstention from food, drink and sex. One deals with this contradiction by separating religion from science, head from heart, spirit from body, thought from actual reality.

Indian writers live these contradictions and write about their crises and fragmentation in a language other than their own. And this is another problem – the problem of the multiplicity of languages. One Indian writer describes this problem thus: the Indian is born with one language, learns another, thinks in one, dreams in one, writes in one.

I did not understand what this meant until I met an Indian woman poet named Akeela and asked her about the problem of language in India.

– When I was born, she told me, I heard my mother speaking Punjabi; when I went to school I learned English and when I grew up I read Hindi books. I write poetry in English because I don't remember my Punjabi mother-tongue and my Hindi is not good enough. But I cannot fully express myself in my

English poetry, because I dream and cry in Punjabi, the language of my childhood. I am not happy with my poetry because it's in a language other than my own. This is a general problem in Indian literature and I think it's one of the most important reasons that there is no great literature in India.

I said to Akeela (which means 'the best' in Hindi):

– You may be right, but in my opinion language is only an external vessel in which to put something. When we dream or cry, we don't do it in any particular language. Our dreams and our tears have their own language which is the human mind, but this does not mean that you can write poetry or literature well in a language you have not perfected. Perfection of a language is essential for any artist who writes. When one perfects a language, one can express oneself in it more than in the language of one's father or mother.

Akeela was still a young woman in her forties, but her fine, innocent features were like those of a fifteen-year-old girl. Her voice was as soft and gentle as a child's, but when you looked into her eyes, you were surprised by that deep, intense and time-worn look, like that of an old man of seventy. This was the secret of her charm and power, for it is pain that makes a person. But the true artist is one who turns pain into first-rate art, not only remaining young and strong despite the years, but staying a sensitive and innocent child with experience accumulated deep in the eyes.

– My sister died at the age of five, Akeela said, before I could buy the red sari I'd promised her. My mother died before I had earned my first wages and could repay her for her suffering. My own life is a continual struggle for survival. I am unmarried and will not marry, but I live love.

This morning I felt inexplicably anxious for my young child I'd left in Cairo with my elder daughter. Last night I had a disturbing dream, the details of which I had forgotten by morning, but which left me with feelings of anxiety that made me pick up the telephone and call my daughter.

I did not know I would have to wait fourteen days and nights. Every day the telephone would ring and the Indian operator would say:

– Cairo will be with you in a few minutes.

I held on for a long time, then the voice would come again:

– Sorry. The line to London is busy.

– London? I asked in surprise. What's London got to do with me? I want to speak to Cairo.

The Indian operator said:

– But all lines go via London and the line to London's busy.

At first I was surprised, but then I remembered that the English had colonised India and Egypt for a period. But if the English had left India and Egypt, why was there no direct line between Delhi and Cairo?

Of course, the line to London remained busy. Fourteen days later the voice of my daughter in Cairo came through. I could not hear her clearly and minutes of the conversation dissolved into nothing, without me hearing her or she me.

Indian literature too, like the telephone lines, only reaches Cairo via London. All the Indian literature we read is translated into English in London. Indians too only know Arabic literature through what is translated into English in London. And London only translates the Indian or Arabic literature that it pleases and that corresponds to its view of India and the Arabs. Thus the greatest of Indian or Arab literature is not translated in London. It remains shut up in the local market and does not reach the international one. For this reason too we do not hear about great authors in India in the same way that we hear of authors like Hemingway and Kafka and Faulkner and Steinbeck, although anyone who goes to India and reads the works of some men and women authors in different Indian states discovers that there is some great Indian literature.

Just as colonialism stripped away India's material resources and wealth so it also stripped away its intellectual, literary and philosophical wealth. Just as colonialism stripped away its national pride and respect, so it also stripped away its pride and glory in literature and art and philosophy.

– Haven't you been to Jaipur? they said to me in surprise.

– What's in Jaipur? I said.

– All tourists go to Jaipur, they said.

– But I go where tourists don't go, because I want to discover the real India.

– Then you must go to Jaipur, they said.

Jaipur is surrounded by huge old walls built by former rulers. They resembled the walls of old Cairo, but were bigger. There were eight enormous gates in these walls, one of them the king's gate through which tourists cannot enter and which are still reserved for the sons and daughters of the former Maharaja. It is closed throughout the year and is only opened when one of them wants to visit the museums inside.

The car circled the walls to reach the tourists' gate. The faces of people in the streets and in the shops looked less weary and more healthy than in other cities. I learned that Jaipur was one of the richest cities in India because of its precious stones. But most of the faces were covered in pockmarks and blotches showing that smallpox had been widespread here years ago. The streets too were covered in red blotches and from time to time, I noticed men spitting out the red spittle of the betel leaf. When one of them opened his mouth to speak or yawn it was red. Sometimes the lips were red inside and outside as though stained by a dye or pouring blood. This strange custom is practised by men (and some women) all over India. You'll see a man sitting and chewing something. Soon you see red spittle running from the corner of his mouth. At first I was astonished to see men's lips red inside and the red blotches in the streets of India.

They say that when one chews the betel slowly one feels full, a false fullness with which the poor of India combat hunger and lack of food. It became a common custom because it contains a narcotic that causes this feeling of fullness. It is addictive. I chewed the thing once but felt no pleasure. This is natural, for such substances need to be taken often to become a habit.

We entered a huge gate into an enormous palace, like those of the Shah in Shiraz in Iran or of the Czar in Leningrad. I had not imagined that the Muslim emperors who ruled India had lived a life such as this. Perhaps they wanted to create heaven on earth, since the iniquity of their actions and their oppression of poor Indians would ensure their entry to hell.

And yet they managed to triumph over hell on earth; summer

in India burns like hellfire but inside these palaces, you find whole rooms built of pure marble that stay as cool as ice, despite the heat. They also put pipes in the walls through which flowed water that evaporated and humidified the air.

Some of the palaces in Jaipur have become universities and institutes or hotels and some have remained as monuments for tourists to look at.

We stopped at one of the palaces that had been turned into a hotel called Ram Baj. *Ram* means god and *baj* means garden. The hotel walls were etched with marvellous engravings and hung with antique paintings and pictures of the Maharaja. The garden was magical and in it one felt transported into an imaginary world of colours, perfumes and flower beds. Between the bushes appeared a number of coloured peacocks that strutted among the flowers, displaying their brilliant multicoloured tails.

Our bedroom was also magical, the ceiling engraved in silver and gold. I told my husband I would find it hard to fall asleep in such a room. Since I could not get to sleep I went to take a warm shower, but discovered that the bathroom was just as magical. It was like the Maharaja's bathroom we had seen at the start of the day; the water taps were silver and the colours of the walls and ceiling made my head spin. I did not enjoy the warm shower much because I was unused to such a life; I imagined the water coming out of the taps had turned into silver or gold threads that electrocuted the body. When I left the bathroom I saw my husband had put on shorts and was jogging around the room. He laughed and said:

– I haven't jogged for days and this room is larger than a sports field.

So I too put on shorts and began jogging.

The bed was like the bed of a Maharaja. I approached it fearfully. Laughing, my husband said:

– I could never fall asleep in a bed like this!

We sat up the rest of the night looking at the bed and the walls and the engravings as though we were in a museum. We only fell asleep with the light of dawn. In the morning we took our cases and hurriedly left the palace.

*

The city of Ahmadabad in the state of Gujarat on the west coast of India is not on the tourist path. Ahmadabad has no Maharaja's palaces or red forts, no tombs of marble or famous gardens or magical lakes, none such fascinating sights. It is a poor and dusty town with hot winds that carry sand from the bed of a huge river that is completely dry in winter and becomes a wide sandy depression. Spread out above it are huts of straw and corrugated iron in which live the seasonal workers who take the sand from the river bed to huge 'Tata' lorries.

Ahmadabad was the cradle of Gandhi's mission. From here, he began his struggle for the poor and lived and died in poverty. I entered the simple house in Ahmadabad in which he lived and from where he set out on his long march against poverty and oppression. In Gandhi's house I saw only his personal effects which were as he had left them before his assassination. I saw the low drum-shaped table at which he sat on the ground writing and reading, beside it his glasses, his book still open, his pen and stick and wooden clogs and sandals, his plate and spoon. This was all Gandhi owned in his life and all that was left after he died.

I stood for a moment contemplating the meagre belongings of one of the greatest leaders in history. I was convinced that Gandhi was faithful to his mission and merited leadership of the great Indian people. I compared Gandhi's belongings with those of other leaders in other countries who claim to fight for rights and equality and justice in their lives but who at death possess thousands of millions in banks inside the country and abroad and whose sons and daughters and wives possess the same or even more.

I found something else in Gandhi's possessions: the small loom on which he wove his clothes and which he took with him on travels abroad. On the wall was a picture of Gandhi weaving on board a large ship bound for England, paying no attention to the blue European eyes that stared at him in astonishment and disdain.

He travelled to England in the white robes which he wove by hand and the shawl which he made on his loom at home and in his open-toed sandals. Like this, stick in hand, Gandhi sat amongst the English in their wool suits and leather shoes and expensive cravats. He sat with them, disregarding their looks, knowing that under the skin were bandits and thieves who were sucking dry his country's resources.

At the start, his mission was only to combat oppression and poverty with love and self-sacrifice in work. The English were not content with plundering the wealth of India, but also imposed exorbitant taxes on the Indian people for any and every thing, even salt. Millions of poor people had to pay tax on salt, their principal food. When these poor were unable to pay the salt tax and were threatened with dying of hunger on the pavement, they came together as a movement, which became known as the Salt Tax Movement.

Gandhi was true to his mission and was a real fighter against oppression but he died violently. One young Indian to whom I spoke as I walked around Gandhi's house told me:

– Gandhi was true to his mission, but truthfulness alone is worthless in a world in which domination is based on corruption and lies and treachery. Gandhi's principle was love, but the weapons of love, like the weapons of truthfulness, are no good against adversaries carrying poisonous weapons. Gandhi was a great man but he was a useless politician. He reached the point of agreeing to the partition of India, the fateful decision that was the cause of his assassination.

– Have you visited Gandhi's *ashram*? the young man asked me.

I asked what Gandhi's *ashram* was.

– Those small buildings facing his house, he said.

– Who lives there? I asked.

– About a thousand men, women and children live there as a commune. They share everything and apply all of Gandhi's principles to their lives in the *ashram*. They work and cooperate with each other, are ascetics and celibate.

– So where do the children in the *ashram* come from? I asked.

– They were born before the mother or father joined the *ashram* said the young man. But after joining the *ashram* there is no physical contact between men and women even if they were married beforehand. They are a group of people who have chosen to live a spiritual and contemplative life together and who have managed to overcome physical desire.

– What's the aim of the commune? I asked.

– For people to live as Gandhi did and to strengthen their spiritual and mental capacities.

– Do you belong to the *ashram*? I asked the young man.

– No, he said.

– Why not? I asked.

– I don't believe in some of Gandhi's principles. I believe that some of his ideas isolate people from the world and make a separation between the body and the spirit. This philosophy does not help people to struggle against oppression. Struggle must be attached to life and not detached from it. A fighter must live in his body and mind because he is only human and no more. I respect the strength of Gandhi and the members of his *ashram* in struggling against physical desires but I would rather they directed their struggle to the external world where millions are exploited and are dying of hunger.

– I agree with you, I said to him.

Whoever has visited India, entered its different temples and is familiar with its many religions, knows that the differences between humans are very few and only superficial – differences in external movements and ways of worship or ritual – whilst the core of human beings remains the same.

In Bombay I went every day to five different temples of different religions; into a Hindu temple, a Jinia temple, a Buddhist temple, a church, then a mosque. I was surprised to find great similarities in the internal and external structures of the five temples – domes, pillars and special place of worship. The men inside the temples have specific attire, movements, way of dealing with people or of taking gifts from them. Likewise, the people that visit temples to pray to gods or goddesses have similar movements, even though some pray standing up, some on their knees, others face down, and all of them give something to the men of this temple or religion.

I had read something about the history of religions, how and why they began, how one religion developed from another, but what I read was not what I saw.

I had read about the need of human beings to believe in something; something to explain the unknown phenomena around them, something to which is ascribed the power to do things

135

that humans are incapable of doing. But whoever watches people worshipping in temples realises that this need differs according to cultural, economic and social class. I was struck that most of those who go to temple are the poor and uneducated. When they pray, they close their eyes completely, their features and bodies assuming a posture of total submission and a sort of terror, fear and contrition, even humiliation. When they present their gifts to the men of religion they are always asking for something, either for God to cure them of disease or to be good to them and protect them from some disaster or give them a child or assist them against the plots of enemies. Some of them spend hours in such prayer.

The very few who are educated are always in a hurry. They pray quickly and their movements do not show contrition or humiliation but rather a desire to finish praying as quickly as possible and go on to other more important things. Whilst praying they do not close their eyes completely but keep them half open. They do not give anything to the poor around the temple, neither do they offer gifts except those that are obligatory religious duties. They do not ask God to heal the sick because they use doctors and medicines, but they ask God for other things, depending on their demands in life and their ability or inability to meet these demands.

In India there is also a sector of people who do not go to the temples. They pray at home and say that God is present inside and outside the temples, he does not have a defined place. Some people in India do not even pray, but say that worship is life and that God is the person who works for the good of people, who has attained a high degree of awareness and wisdom and has become master of himself, neither fearing himself nor any external power because it has been subjected to his strong will and its causes have been disclosed by the intellect and by knowledge. This latter orientation is more common to Buddhism than Hinduism, because the Buddha rebelled against Hinduism, against class and against discrimination between people. In Buddhism there is no God. Yet I saw people in Buddhist temples bowing before statues of Buddha and prostrating themselves before him asking for their requests to be granted like those in other temples. I asked a Buddhist about this and he said that those people had not read Buddhism, were ignorant of his teachings and unconsciously imitated others.

The majority of people do not read because they are illiterate. This means that they know nothing of the real philosophy of their religion and its basic teachings. For this reason religion is much exploited in these countries and becomes a dangerous weapon in the hands of men of religion or men of rule or men of colonialism.

True knowledge of a religion requires that one reads it and understands it in order to have true faith in it. Blind imitation has nothing to do with religion. The Buddhist intellectual said to me:

– Before I read what Buddha said I used to go to the temple and kneel before Buddha like these people. But now I have read and understood, I no longer worship anyone.

– But you believe in Buddha? I asked.

– No. I believe in myself and in anyone who discovers himself and his inner power and with it tries to change the external world to the better for others. This is Buddha's philosophy and it is the principle of Buddhism. But only few have read and fewer still have read and understood.

We took a jeep to visit some Indian tribes north of Bombay who work in brick-making. A young Indian accompanied us on the trip. His name was Samanta; he was thirty-three years old and had studied chemistry in Poland, then had returned to India and worked in a chemical factory in Baruda.

The jeep drove for hours along sandy or rocky roads full of holes and ditches. It was very hot and I would have asked to go back had it not been for the conversation between the young Indian and myself along the way. I noticed that he wore a thread of some sort around his neck. When I asked him about it he said:

– A man puts on this thread before marriage so as to be holy. Before then he can do anything he wants, can have contact with any woman. But after he puts it on he becomes holy and must not approach any woman other than his wife. He never removes this thread as long as he lives.

– Do women also wear such threads? I asked him.

– No. Women never become holy, he said.

– Why not?

– Because they are women.

– What prerogatives does a man who wears this thread get?

– He becomes holy.

– What does that mean? I asked. Is their anything special about it?

– Yes, he said. A holy man has the right to call up the spirits of the dead. I can call up the spirits of my maternal and paternal ancestors. But one person cannot call up more than the seven ancestors of his father and mother.

– What do you do after you've called up the spirits of your ancestors? I said.

– I speak to them and they speak to me and they tell me many things about my life.

– So a woman can't call on the spirits of her ancestors.

– No, he said fervently. Her husband does it for her.

I stifled a laugh and said:

– If I were the wife, I'd call on the spirits of my ancestors by myself.

– The spirits do not answer women, he said.

The logic of such an educated young man surprised me. But I was not very surprised for I'd seen many educated people believe in strange dogmas.

– Don't you ever ask yourself why the spirits answer men but not women? I asked him.

– No, he said. That's the nature of life.

– Who told you so? I said.

– My family. My mother and father and everyone around me.

– But do you inherit the beliefs of your family without revising your thoughts on them in the light of your new studies?

– I studied chemistry, he replied. There's no relationship between chemistry and religion or beliefs, is there?

– There *is* a relationship, I said. There has to be a relationship between anything we study and the ideas and beliefs we inherit. This separation of what we call science and beliefs leads us into many contradictions. Are you married now?

– Yes, he said.

– Did you choose your wife? I asked.

– No, we don't choose our own wives here. Our families marry us.

– Did you have a wedding party? I said.

– Yes, I had my wedding party at four o'clock in the morning.

– Four in the morning? I exclaimed. Why?

– The time of the wedding party is set by the groom's stars and mine was set at four in the morning.

This young man kept on telling me strange stories until we reached a village, where I met one of the Indian tribes.

The tribe reminded me, from my readings in ancient history, of the stone age. Under a tree I saw a brick around which they danced and I learned that this brick was God. They wore a white cloth around their waists and carried bows and arrows and sometimes guns. They did not follow any system or any ruler, nor did they believe in tomorrow or in settling, but worshipped something called freedom. Each one believed himself to be king and no one had authority over him. If they trusted you, they respected you and gave you everything they had, but if they did not trust you, you had better watch out!

It was my good luck that when they looked at my face they trusted me and offered me their food (they are vegetarians and don't eat meat). I ate with them and drank water from the well from which they drink. One of them dipped his finger in a holy red liquid and put a red spot on my forehead. The young man whispered in my ear so that no one from the tribe should hear:

– If the Muslims saw this red spot on your forehead they'd be very angry. It's against Muslim tradition here.

The men and women of this tribe worked as tree cutters. Their houses were of mud and the roofs of branches. On their heads they wore huge turbans, a long strip coiled many times around the head which they uncoiled and tied onto buckets to lower into the well. Their customs are different from those of city dwellers. Men and women have the same sexual freedom before marriage; girls, as well as boys, are encouraged to have relationships before marriage, but afterwards the woman marries one man and the man one woman. Men and women alike were adorned with metal rings on their foreheads, noses, ears and feet. They had a distinctive drum beat which carried me into a different world, as if I'd gone back in time and landed in some primitive age. I felt comfortable amongst them even though I sat on a lump of brick and drank water from the well. It was the comfort we feel with those people who are not false and who do not lie.

The jeep brought us back to town as the sun was setting in the west behind the trees. On the side of the road were banana trees, fields of yellow flowers, sugar cane, wheat and castor-oil, while crows, doves and birds circled in the sky. Between the dense trees I caught sight of lizards, small foxes and monkeys, some playing and some sitting in the trees watching the road attentively like humans.

A mother monkey, her children playing around her, walked with slow steps like a dignified old man. The young monkeys punched each other and played together just as our children do. When I looked at the mother, I found her looking at me. Her movements and voice were human. I stopped the car because I wanted to talk to her as she sat with her elbows on her knees. Her eyes were human, apart from a frantic, startled look, but when she saw that I would not harm her and was approaching her simply to look, her body relaxed and that watchful look vanished. Then she turned her back on me and walked slowly towards her children.

I realised that animals, like humans, need to trust you and be sure of you, otherwise take care!

We had supper with some Indian supervisors of a chemical factory and an American economist working in India, called Fishman. I sat silently listening to the conversation between Fishman and one of the Indian men. They began discussing the Watergate issue, Nixon and the problem of espionage. I heard Fishman say to the Indian:

— I don't understand politics and don't try to understand them. I only deal in economics.

— Is it possible to separate economics from politics? asked the Indian.

— Every science has its specialists, said Fishman.

— But economics activate politics said the Indian, and it's not possible to separate the two.

— But I can't read about Watergate and espionage, then about economics. There are only enough hours in the day for one thing. It's important that I master the branch in which I specialise rather than splitting my efforts into many branches. We have a saying in English: Jack of all trades, master of none.

The Indian replied:

– That's why politicians dominate the world. They understand everything and excel at nothing, which is why they rule and control economics and direct them as they want, in their own, narrow class interests, against the interest of the majority of people.

– I dislike politicians, said Fishman, and avoid talking politics.

With Indian obstinacy and persistence the Indian said:

– But you can't avoid them as long as you work in the field of economics because you actually carry out their policies in that field.

– I'm like a doctor who treats the sick, whether they're friends or enemies, said Fishman.

– No, the Indian said. There's a difference between medicine and economics. Economics are not only an integral part of politics but are the pillar on which politics stand. But medicine is a science separate from politics, isn't it, doctor?

The Indian man directed his question at me.

– Medicine too, I replied, is inseparable from politics. Here a doctor may treat the sick without exploiting them, there a doctor treats the sick and does exploit them. Nothing is separate from politics, not even love.

I learned that Indian men and women workers on tea plantations work nine hours a day for four or five rupees, and produce in one day fifty rupees' worth; that is, ten times the wages they get. Where does the exertion of these men and women go? It goes to the owners of the companies that manufacture and distribute the tea; that is, it goes into the pockets of a handful of wealthy people who exploit the labour of millions of men and women workers.

The vast profit that they make and that they fritter away on luxuries for their wives and children, vanishes into thin air. If only these Indian men and women workers thought for a moment about what their work produced in those nine continuous hours under the burning sun. But they do not think.

We flew on to a small town named Anand in the state of Gujarat on the west coast of India. Although it's small, it is famous. Every packet of cheese in India is stamped with the word Anand. The cheese factory in Anand is owned by a large Indian company that makes cheese, butter and dried milk for children.

We followed the cheese-making process from the moment the buffalo or cow is milked to when the milk becomes a packet of cheese sold in the market. The process is carefully controlled, the machinery in the factory is regulated and the chief engineer explained to us how they had begun using electronic machinery in industrialisation.

But my mind wandered off. I watched the long row of peasant women standing beside the dairy, selling the milk to the factory. Each woman carried on her shoulder a hungry, emaciated child in dire need of the bottle milk which she sold. I worked out that the amount of milk a peasant woman sold for one rupee produces fifteen rupees' worth of cheese. Such a peasant woman is not very different from the woman in the tea plantation who works for one hour for a wage and the remaining eight for nothing.

I spoke my thoughts to the chief engineer who laughed and said:

– That's industry the whole world over. If a factory doesn't make a profit, why should its owners keep it running?

– But the owners make profits of thousands, I said. These peasant women deprive themselves and their children of milk and barely make a living.

– Their buffalos also used to be barely alive because of extreme poverty. We found that care of the buffalos is essential for the production of rich milk in abundant quantities. For this reason, we established a special section in the factory to produce fodder to feed the buffalo and increase the fatty content of the milk. We transfer the sperm of pedigree male buffalo into the womb of the cow who then gives birth to a pedigree calf. We have taught the peasants how to put the sperm tube into the cow's womb, and we also raise some pedigree male buffalos.

142

The engineer took us to the buffalo-rearing farm where we saw a group of bulls walking around in circles. I thought they were pulling a water-mill but I didn't see one. The engineer said:

– These are the exercises the bulls do so they don't get fat for lack of movement and weaken their sperm. We feed them top grade food and daily exercise is essential. We also have a highly qualified medical system to care for the buffalos' health, whether here in the factory farm or in the village. Care of a buffalo's health is most important to the factory because it's the buffalo that gives milk.

The engineer took us to the medical section of the factory. In front of the building were a large number of jeeps, a driver beside each one.

– What are the cars for? I asked.

– They're buffalo ambulances, said the engineer. We have a highly skilled ambulance service and a number of veterinary surgeons who have trained in the highest universities and institutes.

I entered the medical section and saw a number of telephones and a special worker who took messages about sick buffalo anywhere in the region. There were veterinary surgeons at the ready to rush by ambulance to a sick buffalo with first-aid bag, modern medicines and all.

The buffalo aid centre was better equipped than many aid centres for humans in many countries, and in this region in particular. The death rate of children and adults rises for lack of health care and the spread of diseases.

The health care of buffalo also included psychological care. They told me they had studied the psychological reasons a buffalo cow gets depressed and produces less milk. One of the reasons was being deprived of her offspring. A veterinary surgeon told me proudly, looking at some recent statistics:

– There has not been one case of contagious disease among the buffalo in the whole region for ten years and their health has improved greatly. The cows have produced ten times more milk in the last five years. All this is due to the activities of the medical section in Anand.

On leaving the factory, we saw through the walls the pink faces of buffalo in excellent health. We had not forgotten the sight of the skinny, wan faces of the mothers and children and my husband said to the Indian engineer, laughing:

– If the transmigration of souls is true, as the Gita says, then I wish to be reborn as a buffalo in Anand.

We laughed till we cried from so much laughter and so much grief.

On the balcony of the Taj Mahal Hotel the Indian waiter bent to put a tea tray before us. His face was brown and slender under a huge white turban and his teeth shone like silver. The tea pot was also of silver decorated with Mogul Islamic engravings.

The sea air filled me with the smell of iodine and a longing for the sea of Alexandria and the dreams of childhood. The sound of singing and dancing and music rose with the smell of Indian incense, burnt sandalwood and musk. Within me, old feelings or impulses awakened that had lain dormant or perhaps been dead since ancient Egyptian times.

My Indian friend Shandri, Professor of History in the University of Bombay laughed silently, like a deep sigh or long whistle. I did not know whether the shake of his head meant yes or no, but his white teeth lit up his brown face with a smile as he sipped his tea loudly. He said quietly:

– The ancient Egyptians used to dance like us, because we Indians . . .

I interrupted him before he could launch into a long monologue about Indians and their culture, which he believed to be older than Egyptian culture, saying with a laugh:

– Maybe the god Shiva did discover dance, but the goddess Isis discovered wisdom and understanding.

Sucking on a pipe from the corner of his mouth Shandri said:

– Let me explain the matter to you from the beginning because . . .

Waving away the smoke that emanated from his nose and mouth, I said:

– Sorry, I can't follow what you're saying with the sound of music and dancing all around. Just look at those thousands of people!

– It's the festival of the god Janeesh, he said.

– Let's go and join them. Gaiety and delight in life, especially if it's communal, is so contagious I can't resist.

We went down into the street, into an array of colours and tunes and dances. Men, women and children thronged the street as far as the shore, right up to the huge gateway that opened onto the ocean, the famous Bombay Gate that resembled the triumphal arch at the head of the Champs Elysees in Paris. But this gate was not a triumphal one. It was built for King George V of Britain to pass under during his first visit to India in 1911, a gateway built as a massive stone bridge for the English king to pass under.

Shandri shook his head, pointing to the gate:

– Kings in India, like catastrophes and destructive floods, had to build bridges to pass under.

– Yes, I said. In the world of politics, a bridge can be built even if no river passes under it.

We walked with the crowd up to the coast. Shandri stopped under the gateway and surveyed the ocean:

– Politics, like history and religion, is a science that calls for imagination. We cannot understand everything in politics or religion with our senses or even with reason, otherwise Janeesh with an elephant's head would not be a god.

A group of dancing men approached the shore, carrying a statue of the god Janeesh with a child's body, distended stomach and elephant's head. They touched the head and stomach for blessing. Behind the men, women's hands reached out to try and touch the god. Bodies crowded around the wooden god. Men's hands raised the god up high then dropped him into the heart of the ocean.

– They're drowning the god Janeesh? I exclaimed.

– Because he is the fruit of sin, said Shandri.

– What sin? I asked.

– The sin of the goddess Pravati with a man other than her husband Shiva.

– You worship him and then drown him? I said.

– Drowning him means drowning the sin. That's why we celebrate this day.

A woman dancing on the shore threw a red flower into the water of the ocean where the god Janeesh had been thrown, chanting repeatedly.

– Why are you not married, Shandri? I said.

145

His brown face paled.

– When I marry, I'll chose a woman who is a servant not a goddess. Servitude teaches a woman to be faithful to her husband even after his death. She throws herself into the grave with him and does not leave him to be buried alone.

– And you as a husband? Would you throw yourself into her grave if she died before you?

He scratched his head and looked at the ground in silence, as if assembling his thoughts or a distant memory, then said:

– Woman is the cause of sin and the cause of death. She is responsible for her husband's death if he dies before her. That's why the gods order us to bury widows with their husbands. If a widow lives after her husband, she brings about depravity and disasters.

– Do you mean that to bury a widow within the same grave as her dead husband is the law of life? I said.

– Do you object to her being buried in the same grave? he asked. Some religons object to women being buried in the same grave as men. They must be buried in separate graves.

I was still on the seashore, under the huge Bombay Gate. In my head were fantasies of childhood, my grandmother's voice in my ear telling stories of sprites and demons, each demon with eight long arms. Shandri's voice was like my grandmother's:

– The gods do not like widows.

– Perhaps they prefer virgins, I said in a childish voice.

– That's right, he exclaimed. How did you know?

– Because I'm a psychologist, I replied, and I understand the psychology of the gods.

– But our gods differ, Shandri said. Shiva is not like Vishnu or Brahma.

– They may differ politically, I said. Shiva may prefer capitalism, Vishnu may be inclined to socialism, but I believe they all agree in their views on women.

Shandri continued to stare at me. His eyes were narrowed, unblinking like my grandmother's. His voice too was hers. The children of Bombay looked at me with large black eyes full of hunger and surprise like the children in my far-off village on the banks of the Nile and my own eyes in the picture of me as a child standing in the first class beside my peers in primary school.

A man came near Shandri as he was dancing, his garments torn and smelling of garbage, his black eyes burning with hunger. His shadow as he danced fell across Shandri's expensive black English wool jacket; Shandri stopped dancing suddenly and shook the shadow off his jacket as though he were shaking off something of a material substance, like brushing an insect off his clothes.

– He didn't touch you, I exclaimed in surprise.

– His shadow touched me and that's enough, he said. My father used to take a bath if the shadow of an untouchable fell on him.

I too moved away from the man. His smell filled the world with garbage and poverty. I remembered the words of Bernard Shaw: 'I don't like the poor, I don't like their smell.' Is there anyone who likes the smell of garbage? Even the gods of India do not like the poor and the untouchables, particularly the gods Brahma and Shiva, although the poor love the gods the most.

– That's the way of the world, said Shandri. The world is oppressive, but the gods are just. They give wealth to the wicked and give faith to the poor. Faith is better than wealth. The poor are outcast in the world because they are oppressed and transitory, but after death they enjoy the favour of the gods.

I jotted down some words on the paper. I folded it and sent it by telegram as though it were my last will and testament.

He opened the telegram sitting in our house in Giza and was surprised. The letters of the words were repeated like a stammer:

I w w w want you, my d d darling, t t to join m m me, y y
you and m m m me, in the s s s s s same g g g grave.
Your faithful wife

During my travels, I did not ask to meet men or women of power. There is hostility between myself and earthly gods. I was astonished at how much more humble real gods like Shiva and Vishnu could be than the false earthly gods. One rupee or a piece of bread were enough to meet the great god Shiva or god of death and destruction. And he, despite his divinity and omnipotence, attached no importance to fine clothes, had no office manager or private secretary, no chamberlain or anyone blocking my path to him.

But those other gods who walk on earth with their feet, only two, exactly like me; these gods I did not think of meeting. In fact, I rather avoided them. I did not even look at their photos in the daily morning papers, for one simple reason: a real desire to meet the new day with an optimistic and open heart.

In recent years I have grown used to not reading newspapers at the start of the day. I hide them under the desk until last thing at night, then I forget them and go to sleep. But the following morning, I see them looking up at me from under the door.

That morning, I awoke early and as usual looked towards the door. To my surprise, there were no newspapers. The floor was shiny and clean and bare. I jumped out of bed, full of sudden happiness. In one fleeting moment, in a flash, I discovered why I love travelling. I wanted to open my eyes in the morning and not see the papers.

And mornings in New Delhi were bright. I loved the Indian sun in winter. It is a strong sun, stronger than any cold wind. But it is not a tyrannical, despotic strength, rather that of the great, self-confident planets, the strength of real gods with many arms, with compassionate and humble hearts that embrace all equally without discriminating between untouchables and maharajas.

The morning sun flooded over me as I sat on the balcony looking at the Mogul domes and listening to the chirping of a bird whom I heard say:

– You've visited India a number of times and lived here for months. You've been north and south, but you can't leave without meeting Indira Gandhi.

A few days after that morning I found myself in a car passing through the large red gateway that led to the government headquarters in the capital Delhi. I saw just one guard at the outer door and just one secretary greeted me with a humble Indian smile, then took me into the office of the prime minister, Indira Gandhi.

She was standing, wearing a sari which made her look taller and slimmer than I had thought. On her face was a smile that was in keeping with the white tuft of hair on her clear straight forehead. At first glance I knew that her face expressed a personality stronger and more distinguished than the pictures of her I had seen in newspapers, magazines and books. She was one of those whose true spirit and personality cameras cannot convey.

Shaking her hand, I felt at ease with none of the discomfort I always feel inside the offices of those who hold power of any kind. I must have smiled at that moment and my body adopted a natural, relaxed position in the seat opposite hers.

Face to face and eye to eye, the feeling of being before a strong woman increased. I had read some books about her childhood, life and struggle before and after the death of her father Nehru. Along with the leaders of India and men and women of her generation, she had taken part in the struggle against colonialism. When she fell in love with a man not of her religion or class (he belonged to the Farsees who worship fire, and was from a poor class), she resolved to marry him, even though her marriage to him violated all Indian traditions. But she set the example that marriage should be based on love and understanding. This act on her part was a revolution in a society based on the strict separation of classes and religions. At a certain period in her life, she almost gave up politics and public struggle in favour of life as a wife and mother, but she did not manage it. The political struggle was in her blood. She was reared on it as a child and had participated in it throughout her youth. Her life had not been easy. A woman without her strength could not have succeeded in leading Indian society, which was still predominantly male-dominated, inside and outside the family; a vast society, full of problems and riches, that had escaped from the grip of colonialism but still suffered its effects. In India there were now around 300 million people who lived on the breadline. Everywhere we saw people sitting or lying on the ground or living inside huts of corrugated iron or straw or sacking, millions of men, women and children whose home was the pavement and who ate, slept, washed and died there.

Indira Gandhi was surrounded by piles of papers on her desk. Her eyes were full of vitality and her smile was so relaxed that for a few moments I almost forgot that I was in front of the woman whom the west called the strongest woman in the world. But it really was Indira Gandhi with that penetrating look in her eyes and that contraction of the muscles of her mouth when she spoke and a face that assumed the sternness and seriousness necessary for those in power.

She began by saying:

The friendship between the Arabs and India is an old one and we must strengthen and constantly renew it. Although some of our leaders, including Mahatma Gandhi, sympathised with the Jews because of Hitler's outrage against them, we have never approved of the way in which Israel was created. The problem of the Middle East (we call the region West Asia) is a European problem that Europe tried to solve at the expense of the Palestinian people. We here in India support the Arab people because they are oppressed and have suffered the same colonialism and exploitation we experienced for long years. In India we suffered from the oil crisis like other countries, but we know that the Middle East problem must be looked at justly and comprehensively. The Arab countries have the right to struggle and liberate their wealth from the grasp of more advanced countries – all developing countries have the right to do this. We in India love peace and our aim is always friendship, the elimination of misunderstanding and hatred.

We are trying to eliminate poverty in our country. The continuation of the problem of poverty does not mean we have failed as a society, but rather that the system of the modern world has failed to achieve justice. The problem of poverty in our country is not because of overpopulation, as they say in the west, but is due to a fault in the world system. In the west they may be angry with me for this opinion of mine, but we in India understand our problems and the real reasons for them. We realise that industrialisation and comprehensive development and women going out to work are the most important factors leading to the success of the family planning programme. India has progressed in these fields. The birth rate has declined and the Indian woman works in all spheres. In my work as prime minister, I do not face any problems through being a woman.

Women in India participate in all fields. We have two states in which the ministers are headed by a woman. In every state in India there is at least one woman minister. We have many women members of parliament and party representatives, women judges in various states, and in the villages there are women elected to village councils. In India we have a long and deep philosophy of equality between men and women. Former leaders, like Mahatma Gandhi and my father Nehru and others, always supported the equality of women and men, women going out into political and productive life. Women took part in the struggle before independence and went to prison with the men. Women proved they were capable of work and sacrifice, so after Independence it was natural that women should continue in political work and in production.

My father was a rebel and believed that women were like men, so I never felt any discrimination or oppression as a woman. I took every opportunity in education, work and politics. But my mother was deprived of this and always regretted it. I do not agree with the view that a mother should devote herself to her home and children. A woman can be a mother and worker at the same time. Caring for a child and giving it love does not mean that a woman must be at home all day long. The task of bringing up a child does not depend on the amount, but rather the type of love. There are women who stay at home who do not give their children love. There are women who work and give their children real love in the short time they are with them at home. They can also give their children an independence which helps them mature and benefit from the thinking of others. For this reason, I do not agree with the backward way the Indian woman is portrayed in our films. In real life, the Indian woman is more worthy of respect and more advanced, assertive and positive than in Indian films. We are now encouraging groups of young people to make new, progressive films – but the basic role in developing Indian films must be played by women's groups and popular organisations. Their duty is to enlighten public opinion and make equality between the sexes a reality in people's daily lives, so that it can be reflected in films and so that Indian art can be a true expression of the lives of men and women in India. All the laws make women equal to men, but their application in life and art falls on the shoulders of women's organisations and on women themselves.

I visited these groups recently and found that they are under taking wonderful activities, but I found that each group is isolated from the other and there is no coordination between them. Also, most of the activities are concentrated in the towns and among the middle classes and do not penetrate far enough into the countryside and the poor classes. My efforts are directed towards strengthening the Indian individual, eliminating class distinction and protecting the Indian from becoming a cog in a machine, especially since we are moving rapidly towards industrial progress. We are preparing for boys and girls, and male and female workers, to read outside the established syllabuses, outside work, outside the factory, so as to develop their mental capacities and individual talents. In other words, the worker's mind should not be imprisoned inside the factory nor those of boys and girls inside the school, but they must learn about other cultures. India and Egypt both have a deep-rooted history and similar culture, but we know only a little about Arab literature. We are in need of much effort in the field of translation. The Indian individual must read about the Arab individual without English as mediator between them. I have faith in the future and believe that our link with the Arabs and Egypt will continue to grow'

I left Indira Gandhi's office towards afternoon feeling optimistic. In the evening I kept a supper invitation with an elderly Indian writer who was related to Indira Gandhi but was one of those opposed to her policies. He would not acknowledge any good qualities about her and said:

– It's all fine words. What can we expect from her? In our history widows are bad luck and ruination.

The plates of food were emptied and my chest was filled with pessimism. When I left his wrinkled face remained before me and his voice reminded me of my grandmother's.

I was a six-year-old child. Every night before I went to sleep, she would tell me a story of the monster. She would shake her head wrapped in a black scarf and chant, her eyes half closed:

Terrible, frightful
Each of her fingers was three arms two arms wide
At the tip of each finger, two iron nails like scythes

The spot where she sat was arable land.
She was the first to commit outrage on the face of the earth
and work incense and magic
and proclaim rebellion
Thus did Allah set upon her lions like elephants
jackals like camels
vultures like asses
that killed her and freed the land from her evil.

I hid my face under the covers, whispering to my grandmother:
– Is she a sea-sprite?
– No, said my grandmother, she's a woman of flesh and blood, like me, like your mother, like you when you grow up and become a woman like us.
From under the blankets, I asked:
– What's her name, granny?
My grandmother hissed like a snake:
– Her name's *Inaq Un Iwaj*, one of the daughters of Adam's loin, cursed be she and her mother Eve.

Anything and everything can be seen in India. Even the most disturbing dreams of my childhood I saw in India. Even the strangest, most far-fetched yarns I found in India. All this alongside the most modern scientific institutions, the most advanced factories, the largest percentage of those with high degrees of education, men or women.

It is hard for a foreign eye to perceive the power of the Indian woman. But anyone who has studied the life of the Indian woman knows that Indian women in general enjoy more respect and equality than women in many other countries.

I was unclear about the reasons for the elevated status of Indian women, particularly in South India in such states as Kerala which was far from colonialist incursions and was not invaded by patriarchal western capitalist culture based on the exploitation of woman. The state of Kerala was distinguished by the high proportion of educated people, industrial development, advanced culture, the high status of women and the proliferation of matriarchal families.

I also discovered that one of the reasons for the high political and social status of Indian women was that the Hinduism does not fundamentally discriminate between men and women, that gods in this religion are not only male but also female. Many Indians kneel before the goddesses Pravati or Lakshmi and many others.

I lived in India for some months and travelled from one enormous state to another, visiting temples, farms, factories and universities, in each state meeting with a number of men and women writers and the leaders of numerous parties from the far right to the far left. These trips and meetings prompted me into reading about Indian history and its religions, some Indian novels, stories and poetry. The more I learned about India, the more difficult I realised it was to grasp the diversity of its heritage, numerous cultures, trends and endless contradictions. India and Egypt have much in common. I often forgot I was in a foreign country, especially when visiting ancient Islamic monuments. These represent the most important and outstanding civilisation in the history of India (the Muslims ruled India for three and a half centuries, between 1500 and 1850). But the English occupation of India, which lasted for two centuries, left a stronger mark on Indian identity than on Egypt. One is often surprised by that Indian man who lives in English style, a pipe in the corner of his mouth, speaking English through his nose, wearing an English overcoat in the greatest heat, drinking scalding hot tea at five o'clock, taking his dog for a walk every morning.

But there is also the Indian who is aware of the philosophy of Gandhi and Nehru, who struggled for independence and has lived in independence for twenty-seven years. Following the daily newspapers in India was enjoyable. One felt one was in a democratic country, despite the many problems which the government of Indira Gandhi faced.

History is in constant flux. How many empires have fallen and have been replaced by other countries? Will history repeat itself so that the Third World will rise and the empire of the First World fall?

On a dark, moonless night, I stood in humility before the god Vishnu in the basin of the river Jandak. His image was not that of a human being like the god Shiva, or half-human half-elephant like the god Janeesh, but he has the form of a fruit like a banana, the head shaped like male sexual member resembling an unfolded flower ready for fertility.

It was night, completely dark and moonless. The water of the river was black. The Shalijaram and Tulis flowers swayed and embraced furtively, without anyone seeing them. The river was suddenly filled with new-born flowers that glittered under the light of the stars like thousands of tiny fishes.

In the faint light I saw a tall woman emerge from the river. She had a fish's tail, like a mermaid. Her features were strong and godlike, her eyes black holes like those of Hatshepsut or the goddess Isis. The waters of the river were coloured by dark red mud, like the river Nile. I saw her walk with rapid steps on the surface of the water, as though she were walking on land. Now and again, she would bend and pick up something which she put into the opening of her robe. I stared in astonishment. The god Vishnu or Shalijaram had broken into small fragments and she was trying to put the pieces back together by placing them carefully inside her robe. All the parts of the god piled up under the robe on her chest and stomach. When she raised her head and walked on the water, she looked like a pregnant woman although she was only carrying the god who took a new name: Osoris. The Indian philosopher disclosed white teeth in a very brown face and said, nodding his head in Indian fashion:

– Yes, yes, Shalijaram or Tulis are both mother and father. But the mother turned into a curse and the father became a god. Our gods are sinless even if they disguise themselves in husbands' clothes. But the women is always sinful whatever she does or does not do. This is because the gods have cursed her.

I whispered into the night, still staring at the sinful flowers:
– Male religons began with great injustice.

The greatest injustice in India's history fell on hundreds of thousands of Indian women who were raped in the wake of the armed battle. The gods disguised themselves as soldiers, took up English weapons and Indian features and attacked the town on a dark, moonless night. The town was Indian but after partition, it was in East Pakistan. The armed soldiers entered the town, slaughtered the men and raped the women.

Woman is sinful (according to holy teaching) whatever she does or does not do, whether she wants or does not want, whether she is raped by the force of English arms or by any other force of foreign or multi-nationality.

At that time, the gods did not know anything about multinational forces, but they did know one thing: if a woman was pregnant without knowing the father, she was sinful.

In court, the god Vishnu dressed in the guise of a Pakistani judge who stared at the bellies of hundreds of thousands of women impregnated by unknown fathers. The whites of his eyes turned red, as though he were looking at hell. He banged his iron hammer on the wooden table and shouted in alarm:

– Hundreds of thousands of bellies carrying hundreds of thousands of enemy foetuses. They must all be destroyed!

The conscience of humanity was roused. How were the women to blame? How were the innocent foetuses to blame?

The conscience of the priests in the temples and of men of religion around the world was moved. They suddenly remembered that there was something called 'forgiveness' and that the gods sometimes forgive the sin of those whom they want to forgive. One of them shook his long white beard and said:

– Yes, sometimes, and this time could be one of them. The foetuses are doubtlessly innocent and should not be killed. Some of the women who fought to the death against being raped may also be innocent. Thus death saved them from being raped by the enemy. We must ask forgiveness for these innocent women who died defending their honour. But those who stand before us now with bellies swollen by sin, there is no mercy for them and they must be executed forthwith!

Another man shouted:

– But your honour said that the foetuses were innocent and must not be killed. If the mothers are executed, the foetuses in their wombs will be killed too and this is an injustice on innocent souls.

The man scratchèd his long beard, cracked his fingers, then said:

– Yes, yes, what you say is right. The death penalty can be postponed until after the birth.

One of the men sitting on the platform scolded:

– No, that's unacceptable, even dangerous. There will be hundreds of thousands of illegitimate children in our country and not only illegitimate, but all of them the offspring of enemies. Sooner or later, they will look for their fathers and naturally become like them, our enemies!

Silence fell in the court. Then the judges rose and walked off, tripping over the tails of their robes, their long beards shaking on their chests. They vanished into the deliberation room, then returned happy with the solution they'd found. The most senior of them banged his metal hammer and shouted:

– The hearing is postponed to next week to study and consult with American experts!

The Indian men stared in astonishment. What had American experts to do with such a very private matter as this that related to the honour of hundreds of thousands of their women?

However, the press answered these men's questions. Articles appeared by American experts on modern methods of abortion. Even though abortion is forbidden by all religions, it is sometimes permitted.

An extraordinary ruling was issued for mass abortions to kill hundreds of thousands of foetuses. One man with a real conscience asked: Why kill innocent foetuses? but no one replied. The decision was carried out under the cover of night.

One mother refused that her foetus should be killed and they sentenced her to death. The reasons for the ruling were that she had disobeyed the gods and loved her sinful child, offspring of the enemy. A mother cannot love her child and hate its father.

Thus the curtain was drawn over the tragedy of 1971 in India's history following the partition resolution. Another tragedy would sacrifice thousands of Indians before English colonialism finally bid farewell to the most important colony in Britain's slowly crumbling empire.

This is the voice of Amrita Bartiam, the poetess of Punjab and Bengal. Between us in her small house in New Delhi is a tea tray:

– The English ruled under the cover of religious unity. They divided my country and my people into two, one part India, the other Pakistan. The largest migration and slaughter in history took place. Muslims in India were forced to migrate to Pakistan, and non-Muslim Indians had to move from Pakistan to India. On the way, thousands of the two groups were slaughtered, each group defending its own god. If there were no gods, English colonialism would have created them to tear the Indian people apart.

Slaughtered, factional Beirut came to mind. I recalled the words of Marion, my American friend. In our universities, we have secret service operatives looking for means to exploit religions and minorities to create factional discord and divide the country on the basis of religions and gods.

The blood rose to the face of the old English owner of the Indian tea company as he shouted in defence of the holiness of the gods, sipping the vintage wine from a crystal glass, exhaling the smoke of his Havana cigar into the faces of the others. He moved from defending the gods Vishnu and Shiva to accusing Indira Gandhi of disobeying the gods by remaining alive after her husband's death, and not only living but taking power and depriving the Indian people of their freedom.

I stared into the small blue eyes and asked in surprise:

– It seems you are very religious and very concerned for the freedom of the Indian people!

He in turn stared at me, then said in a godly voice:

– Yes. We English are religious and we respect all religions and are concerned for democracy for all peoples, especially the Indian people with whom we are linked by a long and deep history of close friendship.

Amrita said quietly:

– Yes, close friendship and long history sanctified by the purged blood of martyrs.

The owner of the Indian tea company raised his voice, saying:

– Yes. Let us all pray for the souls of the unknown martyrs and call upon them for forgiveness and mercy and entry into heaven, amen.

Then he poured the rest of the wine down into himself.

PART EIGHT

*The City
of Worship
and
Debauchery*

The plane circled in the sky above Thailand. Beneath the huge steel wings, the lights of Bangkok looked like thousands of beads on a pearl necklace. As the wheels of the plane touched the ground lightly, as though gliding on water, dance music came from the speakers in the roof of the plane and I nodded my head in time to the tune. An old man with grey eyes stared at me from under his glasses.

Bangkok airport was spacious and modern, like any airport in Europe or America. A white car bearing the United Nations emblem was waiting for my husband, the driver a Thai who opened the car door for us with a deferential bow.

I glanced at the driver's face from the side. From time to time he glanced at us furtively through the small mirror as we sat in the back seat.

His closed lips opened suddenly as he said in English with an American accent:

– Bangkok has become a part of America. We got American experts everywhere.

He pointed through the car window towards the huge aeroplanes.

– Great American war planes! He nodded his head in pride and asked: you two from America?

– No, I said.

His lower lip fell in disappointment and he asked: Where are you from?

– We're from Egypt, my husband replied.

– Are there many Americans in your country too?

– No, I said.

– Who do you have? he asked.

– We have Egyptians, I said.

His eyebrows arched in surprise, then lowered quickly, as if he had suddenly discovered that the matter did not call for surprise. His lips closed, but he looked at us now and again in the mirror as though we'd landed from another planet or belonged to an alien species.

The car stopped in front of a hotel that resembled any Hilton or Sheraton in any world capital; a hotel without identity or personality or character, like a blank coin. We decided to leave it early the following morning, before sunrise.

At the outer door of the hotel, a small man who looked much like the driver of the previous day, approached my husband and whispered something in his ear that I could not hear. I saw my husband wave him away, saying: no, thank you!

The man did not go away but clung to my husband.

– What's he saying to you, I asked.

– He says he has a beautiful woman for me tonight!

When the man approached again, I said to him:

– Don't you have a beautiful man for *me* tonight?

His narrow eyes widened in astonishment, then he sped away.

Buddha was the deity here, sitting cross-legged, a statue of bronze, a serpent on his head. The serpent in Buddhism symbolises protection and water (or goodness).

Only a small minority here, seven per cent of the people, believe in the Indian god Shiva. He squats on stone statues in the shape of a huge male member, surrounded by infertile Hindu and Buddhist women. The infertile Buddhist woman believes in any god that can grant her fertility, whether it is Buddha or Shiva or even the god of children, Janeesh, with the elephant's head.

The faces of barren women were pale, the colour of grey callico, their eyes raised towards the god, chapped hands lifted; their lips opened, chanting words I did not understand.

I asked the priest: Is it a supplication to god?

The priest looked into my face with small eyes and said:

– What god? We don't have gods like the Hindus. Buddha is

not a god; he is a holy person whose teachings are holy, but he did not call himself a god.

It was Sunday, market day in Bangkok. Small shops like square boxes lined the roadside, thousands of foreign tourists jostled to buy Thai silk, the best and the cheapest in the world. The labour of workers in the silk factories was still cheap; thousands of poor girls stood at machines sixteen hours a day (from six in the morning to ten at night). A girl's daily wage was two and a half dollars, seventy-five dollars a month, nine hundred and six dollars a year.

The factory girl did not make in one year what a prostitute made in one week, or half a week, or sometimes in one night.

But a prostitute here was not called a prostitute. And brothels here were not called brothels. They were called 'massage parlours' and were no less respectable than medical clinics and certainly more important and numerous.

The massage parlours competed to attract foreign tourists and the state encouraged them; they bolstered the national wealth with hard currency. This was a patriotic duty.

But the problem, as one masseur told me, was that the massage parlours increased faster than the foreign tourists. The competition between them had grown intense and each parlour hired men called 'tourist guides' whose task was to hunt male tourists in the hotels or pick them up on the streets! I would see them standing at the doors of hotels and on street corners, their eyes darting in all directions. As soon as they saw a tourist, they'd pounce on him:

– I've got a beautiful woman for you tonight. Our prices are the cheapest; service includes everything; massage of stomach, thighs, legs, between the legs, finger cracking. We've got the most beautiful Thai women and the most beautiful women in the world. We've got all nationalities, of all sizes, and also virgins for whoever wants to be the first.

Curiosity overcame me – I wanted to see one of these parlours from the inside. But women, except those who work there, were forbidden to enter: their role was solely to provide a service whereas consumption was the sole right of men. I disguised myself in men's clothing and went in search of a massage parlour.

Inside, backs bowed before me in deference, eyes looked at me with utmost respect. For the first time, I understood what it meant to be a man.

I raised my head in pride and imagined I was a man. I found myself standing in a row of men, shoulder to shoulder, our feet touching, eyes forward.

Rows of girls sat before us behind a pane of glass, like small animals imprisoned inside glass cages, like goods on display behind shop windows. We could see them without them being able to see us, legs naked and white, jutting breasts from which hung numbers, like the numbers of prisoners. Staring eyes fixed on breast or leg and ran like slivers of glass over the chalk-white, soft flesh, the faces of white plaster dolls. On each cheek was a circle of red like a stain, eyes were raised for a moment in a furtive glance, a glance filled with emptiness that was like sadness or sadness filled with emptiness.

The girls' bodies were as small and slender as children's, the men's as large as rhinoceri or dinosaurs. A tall man suddenly lifted his hand and pointed to a number on the chest of one of the girls. Beside the number was the price also in the form of a number. She jumped up like a moth touched by light and walked on tiptoe down a long passage, at the end of which was a closed door. She opened the door and went in, and he entered behind her. Then the door closed.

I was confused and hesitant. Should I raise my hand and point, or not? Perhaps my hand did move – through my hesitance – and draw attention, for one of the men came bowing towards me, in his eyes a look of utmost respect:

– Can I help you? Anything you need, sir?

– No, thank you, I said.

I forgot that my voice was not that of a man. The man's eyes bulged in astonishment and the look of respect quickly vanished. He took me to the parlour manager.

The manager's small, slim body appeared from behind a huge desk as he stared at me in surprise and said: you lost your way and came in here by mistake, didn't you?

– No, I said. I came to satisfy my desire for knowledge, my curiosity.

The blood rushed to his face and he slammed his fist on his desk in anger:

– Curiosity! Don't you know that a respectable person does not give in to curiosity? This is a reputable place – he banged on the desk – yes, reputable, and there is no place here for the satisfaction of disreputable desires.

– A man's sexual desire may be more reputable than a woman's desire for knowledge, I said, but the god Shiva created all desires, including the desire for knowledge!

– I do not believe in the god Shiva, shouted the man.

– In which god do you believe? I asked. Buddha also respected curiosity and did not separate it from the desire for knowledge.

– I am not a Buddhist, the man answered angrily. I am Jewish and I believe in the Torah!

I stared at him in surprise. I thought that only Buddhism or Hinduism existed here.

– I have the right to call the police, said the man.

I smiled sarcastically.

– Of course, that's your right. You've caught me redhanded, committing a sinful desire – the desire for knowledge.

He seemed not to have heard me, but was deep in thought. Then he looked at his watch, jotted some numbers on a piece of paper, added them up and wrote down the total.

– You can pay me seventeen and a half dollars as a fine and go free.

– That's robbery, I said angrily.

Very quietly he said: that's our right. You came here to obtain knowledge. That's seventeen and a half dollars for the knowledge you've got. I don't open this place for people to come in and get what they want for free. Nothing's free in this house. Besides, my time costs money and you've taken up nine and a half minutes of my time.

I thought for a minute. The logic of this man was sound in the language of the market and trade. He was a man of the market, selling sexual gratification to respectable men by the minute, according to the sheet dangling before me. It looked like a list that might hang in a doctor's surgery. If the price for gratifying the desire to crack the fingers and feet was one and a half dollars per minute, how about gratifying the desire for knowledge? If he wanted seventeen and a half dollars from me for nine and a half minutes, he was calculating one minute at about one and a half dollars, in other words, the same price as for the cracking of fingers and feet.

– In any case, I said to myself, it's to my advantage that the price of knowledge is cheap.

I was on the point of paying the seventeen and a half dollars when I reminded myself that this house was one of prostitution, under the name of a massage parlour, and that this man exploited girls to make his money. I found myself saying to him angrily:

– I will not pay you one cent! It is I who will take *you* to the police – this is a brothel, not a massage parlour!

The man began to retreat:

– We don't do anything illegal.

His voice got lower, his back bent, and with a polite bow he saw me to the door.

It was easier for me to enter a temple than a massage parlour. The priests did not forbid anyone from entering, as long as one paid something, food or clothes or money, to the gods. For the gods here, like humans, needed money and food and clothes. True, all these things ended up with the priest in the temple, but the priest deputised for the gods and there was no separation between the property of the priest and that of the gods.

In front of the temple, I saw a Buddhist priest with shaven head and a long saffron robe sprinkle holy water on the ground, then hold out his hand to people saying:

– Donations for the gods.

He held out his hand like a beggar.

Early each morning, these priests come out in their saffron robes and shaven heads, their hands outstretched, begging for their food. You met one in every street. A priest might be away from the temple for three days or more on a begging journey, then return to the temple with enough provisions to last for a week or month. If supplies ran out, he would set off on another journey to get food.

The priest shared with me a fruit called durian, a popular fruit of Thailand. I took a bite: it had a delicious, apple taste but it smelled awful. I put a handkerchief to my nose as I ate it.

– Let the smell enter your chest, the priest said. It's good for your health.

– You're a priest, who understands religion, but health is my field because I'm a doctor.

– I'm also a doctor, replied the priest.

I learned there was a medical school inside the temple where the priests trained in acupuncture and other similar disciplines. They were called barefoot doctors.

In the corner of the temple I saw an opening in the ground shaped like a trough that stored holy water for washing the Buddha's feet. His feet were imprinted on a piece of stone which some women were kissing while the priest sprinkled them with holy water, murmuring:

– Purify them from sin!

The priest wanted to purify me, too, and sprinkle me with holy water, but I refused. I did not want to catch a skin disease. I said to the priest:

– I did not enter the temple for purification.

– Why did you come? he asked me angrily.

– Simple curiosity, I said.

– This is a reputable house of worship, not a place for sinful desires, he shouted in anger.

– Buddha did not forbid curiosity or the desire for knowledge, I said quietly.

– Then pay Buddha something for revealing knowledge.

I took some money out of my pocket and left.

PART NINE

African
Journey

My journey to Africa was belated. I saw Europe, America and Asia before I saw Africa, even though Africa is the continent in which I live, and our roots and the sources of our Nile grow from its heart.

But our eyes and our faces were always turned towards the Mediterranean, Europe and America, our backs towards Africa, away from ourselves. When one turns one's back on oneself, when one is ashamed of one's brown or black skin and tries to hide it with white make-up, how can one know oneself? The evil of European colonialism was to bleed Africa of her resources and wealth, but the greater evil was that arrow with which the white man wounded the African identity, so that being African became a shameful blemish and a black skin a contract of slavery. My journey to Africa lasted three months, in the summer of 1977; not long enough to enter into the heart of the African, but enough at least to enter into my own heart and learn about myself and about my being African.

The first aspect of my Africanness is the brown colour of my skin which turns black after some days in the sun, so that walking in the streets of Ethiopia or Uganda, hardly anyone notices that I'm a foreigner. I must admit that this does not always please me, for deep inside me, stemming from childhood, is a longing to be as white as cream. I still remember, despite the passing of the years, that ever since I was born, as a child I was certain of two things: firstly that I was a girl and not a boy like my brother and secondly that my skin was brown and not white like my mother's. With these two facts, I realised something even more important: that each of these two characteristics was enough to doom my future to failure. The only quality which prepared a girl (at that time) for a secure future was being beautiful, or at least as white-skinned as the Turks.

My maternal grandmother, who was of Turkish origin, used to tease me by calling me 'Slavegirl Warwar' . . . . From then on, it was fixed in my mind that slavegirls and slaves had skin the colour of mine and I began to hide it with white make-up, imagining that the action of hiding my skin was a move towards something better. And yet, another side of me realised that the colour of my skin was as real as my being a girl. And I love the truth. The one true love of my life is the love of my real self. In spite of that, I only gave up make-up completely after I understood the worth of my mind, and then had the courage to face the world with a clean and washed face.

I would sit with African women and men in Dar es Salaam, their skin as black as burned milk or cocoa, tall and erect in stature, the natural movement of their walk like dancing, their eyes when they talked like singing, their songs of love like their songs of revolution, the word 'freedom' in the Swahili of East Africa like our Arabic word *al-huriyya* with a slight change of pronunciation. I loved their accent and sang *al-huriyya* with them. They told me I was African like them, but Africa had been divided into north and south; this was black Africa, as though North Africa were not Africa, as though there were a black Africa and a white Africa.

I felt relaxed with them and at ease with myself, with my brown skin. The real parts of myself had emerged, filling me with confidence and pride, feelings I had not had on my trips to Europe and American and Asia, feelings which after I experienced them, made me regret that my journey to Africa came so late.

I now had a comfortable feeling of familiarity with myself and with the brown colour of my skin, a familiarity I had never known so clearly before. I have not forgotten that on my first journey to America in 1965 I stood in front of a mirror in North Carolina before entering the toilet, for I had read the sign 'Whites Only' on one door and 'Blacks Only' on another. That day, I stood in front of the mirror confused as to which door to enter. My skin was neither white nor black but somewhere in between and I did not know to which world I belonged.

My Tanzanian friend, Paris, laughed. She is a professor of economics at the University of Dar es Salaam and told me:

– I studied in England in 1959 and they made me feel so inferior for being black and a woman that I became ashamed of myself. But I changed a lot after I studied economics and learned how they had colonised us and destroyed our economy and our souls. In my lifetime I am seeing socialism being gradually realised in my country Tanzania and with the passing of the years I understand the strong links between economic justice and the freedom of men and women. In our authentic African heritage there is no discrimination between men and women. Do you know that our minister of justice is a woman?

She gave me the phone numbers of the justice minister both at home and in her office. I said it might be better to call her in the office rather than at home. Paris was surprised and said there was no difference. I soon realised that people in Africa treat ministers and rulers as ordinary people: there are no doors or barriers or conventions. I spoke with the minister of justice in her house and asked her:

– Are you really minister of justice?

She laughed and told me there were women in all fields, ministers and others. I told her we had one woman minister for social affairs, but justice in our country was still the sole domain of men. Talking to the minister of justice, I remembered an article I had read in an Egyptian newspaper last year in which a woman writer had said that there were certain preconditions qualifying a person to take up the position of judge, the first of which was masculinity.

I looked around, walking along the shores of the Indian Ocean in Kenya, Tanzania, Zanzibar, the Seychelles and Madagascar and wondered at the magic I had never seen before. The mountains of Kenya and the towering peak of Kilimanjaro in Tanzania are no less wonderful than the mountains of the Himalayas which I saw in Nepal. The dense green mountains of Ethiopia and Uganda resemble the green paradise around Lake Victoria. The beauty I saw in East Africa I had not seen in Switzerland whose beauty I had often heard praised. The shores and mountains of East Africa were more exotic and green, a combination of mountains, water and dark equatorial vegetation; mango and coconut trees, the strong smell of equatorial flowers, that refreshing coolness in the air – more refreshing that the cold of a European summer.

I used to think that I would fry, travelling in sub-equatorial Africa in August, but I found that, being thousands of feet above sea-level, most of these countries were protected from the heat. The weather was temperate, like springtime in our country, and cooler the higher one got.

The heat in East Africa is in the political climate, and it is a natural heat. Long years of slavery led in the end to a hot revolution which had its advantages and also its dangers. When I said in Cairo that I was going to Uganda and Ethiopia and East Africa, eyes widened in surprise and everyone cautioned me, for revolution was breaking out everywhere. But I was determined to go, for I love to be where people are in revolt and angry. Anger, in my view, is a psychological state suitable to this age. Since primary school, when I first heard about Lake Victoria and the sources of the Nile, I have been determined to go in search of my own sources and roots. My paternal grandfather was called *Habashi* (Ethiopian) and I was told that he was dark-skinned and had Ethiopian blood. When my mother got angry, she would say that I had inherited the skin of my father's family. Was it not my right, after all that, to find out about my roots and sources? As for the sources of the Nile, in Uganda I stood perplexed before the splendour of its high green banks near Kampala, the point of contact between the White Nile and Lake Victoria.

I stood and contemplated the narrow neck of the river at the point of contact with its source. Unconsciously, I raised my hand to my neck and felt in it a strange terror and tremor, for that small narrow neck was an artery in the earth of my body. It was my neck, yet it was not in my body but in another body, Uganda, surging with the violence of the political upheavals of Idi Amin.

On the heights of Ethiopia and in Addis Ababa, about seven thousand feet above sea level, the rains poured down day and night. I understood that these rains carried irrigation and silt to us and I rejoiced at the sound of thunder, saying to myself: these gushing waters will flow into the land of my peasant people.

When my husband, children and I got out of the plane at Entebbe Airport, we realised we were the only visitors to Uganda and the airport staff looked at us in surprise and wonder. Who were these adventurers coming to Uganda at such a tense time? The management of the Lake Victoria Hotel in Entebbe advised us not to leave the hotel after sunset.

In Dar es Salaam and Nairobi they gave us the same advice: don't walk in the streets after sunset. As the days were noisy, full of sun, movement and vitality, so the nights were dark, silent and full of danger. The city of Nairobi in Kenya, built in ultra-modern style, plunged into all the activity of a modern city, but as soon as night fell, the streets were empty of all but thieves. In Dar es Salaam, before the sun sets, you saw Tanzanian boys and girls strolling along the shores of the Indian Ocean, the barefoot girls selling boiled eggs or green mangoes, the boys sitting in front of the buyer peeling the egg for him, then splitting it with a small spoon and filling it with hot pepper. Green mangoes were also cut with a knife and filled with pepper. In the cafés sat women as well as men, alone or in groups, drinking beer, smoking and talking politics. But as soon as the sun set, the streets emptied of people and darkness and silence fell, apart from the small lights that came from the ships anchored in the port.

They say that Nairobi, the capital of Kenya, is the bridegroom of Africa. It is a modern city, although it seemed to me like a groom who has put on a beautiful robe on the outside, but whose undergarments are ugly. I have seen this duality in the capitals of countries which are not liberated or which are only liberated in appearance. Many capitals in our Third World are like Nairobi. I remembered Bangkok when I walked in the streets of Nairobi: the same modern buildings, the same American cars, the same broad tarmaced streets, the same corners on which prostitutes stood, the same American crime and sex films in the cinemas, the same advertisements for Kent cigarettes, Cadillacs, Seven Up and Coca Cola.

I stopped for a moment in front of one of the cinemas, looking at the queues of young Africans, youth completely defenceless against this creeping danger, this flood of cheap art, this evil brainwashing that is perpetrated every day not only in the countries of Africa and Asia, but in America and Europe too: but western youth has acquired a sort of immunity to such danger, due perhaps the relatively higher economic and educational standards of living. Our African young have no weapons with which to protect themselves from this epidemic.

A tall African youth, wearing a chain around his neck and a coloured shirt on which was drawn a heart and the words 'I love New York' in English, smoked a Kent cigarette and chewed gum. I saw him as ugly, the city of Nairobi uglier still. I realised the real insult behind what we call ugliness: it is the contradiction between external elegance and the internal corruption, whether in a person or in a city.

I flew a small plane, a German Volker that was like an old bus with torn seats and propellors that sounded like an antique motorcar. I thought it would fall from the sky as the lights of Dar es Salaam shone under me, the ships in the port glistened like dolls. The plane landed twenty-five minutes later on the island of Zanzibar, a dark and silent island that seemed to hold a closed undiscovered secret. In the airport they gave me four quinine tablets against malaria. They told me that the island was infested with malaria and filaria and tuberculosis. Those suffering from leprosy were quarantined on another nearby island known as the Island of Death.

I stared into the darkness, sitting in the taxi from the airport to the Bwana Hotel. The air was heavy with death. I considered going back to the airport, but the desire to know was strong. I had stepped onto the soil of Zanzibar, the island of slavery, and breathed the smell of enslavement. In the huge hotel on the shore, the bellboy bowed and took my case from me.

In the morning, I lay beside the swimming pool, not daring to go into the water. A smell like death emanated from the depths of the pool and from all over the garden. The bellboy whispered in my ear:

– When we dug up the earth to lay the swimming pool, we found thousands of bodies and human skeletons. They killed the revolutionaries and buried their corpses here before the hotel was built.

I jumped up and went to pack my case, deciding to move to another hotel.

– This is the only hotel on the island, the bellboy said. The others are old and third class. Nobody goes to them because of the malaria and filaria mosquitoes.

– Malaria and filaria are better than staying in this hotel, I said.

I moved to a small hotel in a narrow alleyway, called Africa House, overlooking the ocean. The building was African Muslim in style, with strong and massive pillars like African forearms. The room was clean, the bed was covered by a white sheet and the smell of cloves emanated all around and revived me. The sound of singing and drums filled the air with joyfulness. Children carrying small lanterns walked in the streets singing to the month of Ramadan. It reminded me of the children of my village on the banks of the Nile. The small roadside shops were like those of Moski in Cairo. A child gave me a branch of clover and shook my hand, saying:

– *Qaribou wajini yanju*

I did not understand. A small girl who knew Arabic told me:

– He's welcoming you.

The girl's name was Hoda and she was the daughter of an Egyptian working at the Egyptian Consulate. Her mother came out of a clover shop and shook my hand. Her name was Um 'Ala. She did not have a son called 'Ala, but the whole island was Muslim and they had old customs. They did not call a mother by her name but by her son's name. If she had no son, they invented one for her, simply so that she could carry his name.

She drove me in her small yellow car to her house. On the wall was a picture of the Pyramids of Giza and the Sphinx, and a prayer mat with the picture of the Ka'aba in Mecca. Her features were thoroughly Egyptian, her head like Cleopatra, and the expression in her large black eyes was a combination of strength and sadness. She brought me a tray of tea and small festive cakes and said:

– I have read your books and wanted to come to your clinic in Cairo.

– I closed my clinic years ago, I said.

– Why? she exclaimed.

– I was not happy with the idea of giving people health at a price, I said.

– I spent everything I had on psychologists in Cairo. I suffer from depression, doctor. My drawers are filled with sedatives and tranquillisers. I left my job in Cairo to accompany my husband on his diplomatic life. Twenty years we've been travelling all over the world, from New York to Zanzibar. Hoda, my daughter, lives alone in Cairo throughout the year and we only see her in the summer holidays. My father died when I was in New York and I did not see him. My mother died last year when I was here in Zanzibar. My husband also suffers from depression because he hates Sadat and knows that he does not work for the good of Egypt, but every day he has to say the opposite because of his diplomatic post.

Her daughter Hoda came in at that moment and Um 'Ala stopped talking. Then she changed the subject and said:

– What have you seen in Zanzibar?

– Nothing, I said. Until now I was in the Bwana Hotel under which are buried human skulls.

Um 'Ala laughed.

– I'll take you by car to see Zanzibar museum, which used to be a slave house.

I sat beside her in her small car. Her delicate fingers around the steering wheel were calm and confident. I heard her say:

– Driving gives me self-confidence and makes me feel independent. My whole life I've lived in the shadow of a man, my husband, even in the shadow of an illusory son. I have created for myself another world in which I dream of freedom, as a slave does.

Some children gathered around the car and ran behind us like the village children of Egypt do. Their faces were as pale and thin as those of the children in my village, and covered with flies. Um 'Ala said:

– The island of Zanzibar has many resources and much clover, but the people here do not have meat or vegetables or even water. Everything is imported from Dar es Salaam. The necessities of life are not here on the island, but there are colour televisions and other luxuries imported from Europe and America.

The girls wore long dresses and covered their heads. A girl who wore a short dress in the street, even if she was ten years old, was liable to be imprisoned for anything from three days to six months. The voice of the *muezzin* from the minarets was louder than the sound of the radios and colour televisions.

We reached a small square called Slave Square, in the middle of which was an enormous church like those of the Middle Ages. Its windows had bars and reminded me of the inquisition courts. Behind the church was another building as huge as a palace, built on pillars and surrounded by trees. The walls of the palace were blackened as though from an old fire. The sultan had lived in this palace in 1899 with his *harem* of hundreds of women. The women conspired against the sultan and burned down the castle, then escaped to the ocean in boats. Beside the palace was a tower called the House of Wonders. The aroma of cloves filled the air and the coastline stretched onto the horizon. Tall slender coconut trees reached up to the sky, the dense green leaves of the mango trees waved in the ocean breeze, and waves broke over the rocks that rose from the water as black as the heads of slaves. The slaves' house itself, like the rocks, was a memorial to the time of slavery. The rock dungeon deep inside the building had been a storeroom, where slaves were stored like goods and where they lived with snakes for months.

In the square, the men, women and children were sold in chains in the market. In the small museum we saw the iron chains behind glass. On one piece of iron was a dark spot, like old blood.

We returned to the car with heavy hearts. In Um 'Ala's home at the lunch table, I met her Egyptian husband and two other men, one of them a civil servant named Mahmoud who worked in the Egyptian Embassy in Dar es Salaam, and the second a leader of the nationalists in Zanzibar named Sheikh Ali Muhassan. His face was as strong and sad as an imprisoned lion, a combination of Arab and African features. Arabs and Africans have intermixed in Zanzibar for hundreds of years so that you can hardly tell them apart.

Sheikh Ali Muhassan had fought with his comrades against English colonialism until Zanzibar won its political independence and began to aim for economic independence.

Colonialism did not see much harm in African countries becoming politically independent as long as economically they remained attached to the capitalist market; no country was allowed to escape from its economic grasp. Ali Muhassan and his colleagues were imprisoned in Dar es Salaam. Most of them died in prison, but Ali Muhassan managed to escape and get away with his life.

He said: The English are scared of Zanzibar because the revolution is underground and may spread to Tanzania and other African countries. English colonialism continues to work in secret in Africa, together with America.

A heavy and apprehensive silence fell. The air, too, had grown still. I went to a window overlooking the ocean. The Island of Death, where they abandoned leprosy sufferers to the hyenas and snakes, signalled from afar. Between the dense trees I saw the pillars of the burned palace and the Bwana Hotel where thousands of revolutionaries had been buried under the swimming pool; then Slave Square where the chains and the rock dungeons were.

From the island of sadness and slaves, I flew to Dar es Salaam and from there to the island of Madagascar, which they call the Island of Smiles. The plane landed in the middle of the road, on an island in the middle of the ocean called the Seychelle Island, a strip of green land set in the midst of the water, waves and rocks. The features of the people were a mix of Arab and African blood, their unintelligible dialect a mix of Swahili and Arabic. White moonlight reflected on white robes, the whole island was enveloped in a sort of magic and behind the beauty was the smell of intrigue and smuggling.

From the Seychelles, the plane took me to Tananarive, the capital of Madagascar, known as the city of a thousand fighters and a thousand houses. Its small white houses with sloping red roofs were built on the hills and were gradually covering upper and lower slopes. Its people had fought the Portugese, the Arabs, the English and the French and finally gained independence in June 1960. The women fought alongside the men, worked in all fields and had the same rights as the men.

Young men and women walked arm in arm on the shore that

led to the main street, Independence Street, in the centre of town. At the end of the street was a market called *al-Zouma*, the word taken from the Arabic *al-Joum'a* (Friday market), with small shops and white sunshades. I saw flowers, fruits, a festival of colours, people wearing large hats of palm leaves and straw, smiling and exchanging greetings, beautiful and perfect handicrafts; a hybrid of Arab, Asian and European cultures.

The people on the island of Zanzibar lived in poverty and sadness whereas here the people seemed more joyful and nature more beautiful. Girls danced the flower dance around the lake, smiling, their dresses fantastic colours. If Zanzibar was the Island of Sadness and Slavery, Madagascar was the Island of Smiles and Joy.

PART TEN

Emperor Haile Selassie and the Revolution

Since Sadat had been in power, I had felt alienated in my homeland. For eleven years, from 1970 to 1981, a black cloud obscured the sun, the light and the breeze. Only his face remained before us and looked down on us every day from our screens, from the pages of newspapers pushed under the door by a hidden hand, his voice thundering from loudspeakers in the streets and broadcasts.

Every time I saw or heard him, I felt alienated. And the alienation was accompanied by a feeling of falling into a dark well in which human rights had been lost.

Everything was upside down in our lives; danger became security, freedom was dictatorship, martial law became democracy thanks to knowledge and faith. Exhorbitant price rises, debts and inflation took on the new name of prosperity. Military bases and rapid deployment forces became protectors of peace. Concern for peace in Afghanistan paralleled a concern for French interests in Chad and the long struggle against imperialism and Zionism turned into friendship, affection and cooperation.

We began to see Israeli beer and eggs in Egyptian shops. A stream of American advertisements for Kent cigarettes, Seven Up, Schweppes and false eyelashes for women rained down on us. Local goods vanished from the markets, even Egyptian macaroni, rice and bread. The level of unemployment among the young rose, as did voices calling for women to return to the home and put on their veils.

Everything foreign became of greater value than anything Egyptian, even people; foreigners enjoyed more attention and respect from all government officials than Egyptians, from guards at doors to the highest directors, ministers and the head of state. Foreigners, particularly Americans, obtained favours and facilities to establish investment companies or carry out research and get information and data that Egyptians did not.

How bitter it was to feel oneself a stranger in one's own country, when anyone who wore foreign clothes or jabbered in a language other than Arabic obtained respect.

It was not strange, under this regime, that I should be sacked from my job, should have all my writings confiscated, and be forced to live in semi-exile, ending up in prison.

Despite everything, all these experiences were useful and enabled me to travel and see other worlds and to work in another system similar to the government system in our country, called the United Nations Organisation.

I acquired a new title, that of 'expert'. In my pocket was a blue passport on which the glove was drawn, above it *United Nations* and below it *Let Him Pass*.

I passed through all the airports of the world without anyone stopping me. At the end of every month I got three thousand dollars, aside from travel and living expenses, which was three times what my wages had been from the Egyptian government.

My first residence was Addis Ababa, the capital of Ethiopia. I have blood ties to Ethiopia as my paternal grandfather was called *Habashi*–Ethiopian. High on the wall of my maternal grandfather's house hung a picture of the Emperor Haile Selassie. My aunt used to say that her grandfather was a friend of the emperor's and with her long, manicured fingers pull a sheet of paper from the desk, paper that the years had faded but on which remained printed words that proved that the *Khedive* Ismael had loaned and confiscated a piece of land from her grandfather.

I was still a child and did not know the difference between an emperor and a *khedive* – the letters of the name 'Haile Selassie' under his picture looked like hieroglyph to me. He had large eyes in a long thin face, a sharp, pointed nose, and on his chest large brocaded things which my aunt said were decoration sand medals like those of King Farouq. When King Farouq fell in July 1952, I imagined that Haile Selassie would also fall.

I did not know anything about Ethiopia except that it was a

high ridge where rain fell and where the sources of the Nile were.

In 1974, when I read that Haile Selassie had fallen, I was reminded of King Farouq and imagined that Ethiopia had been liberated. But Sadat announced that red devils had taken power in Ethiopia and that the fall of Haile Selassie was contrary to the will of Allah because Allah had chosen him; he was ready to take up arms and go to Ethiopia to defend the will of Allah and also protect the sources of the Nile from the encroachment of the devils.

I believed none of what Sadat said. He himself did not believe what he said and since he realised that people would not believe him, he always resorted to Allah.

The Ethiopian aeroplane covered the distance between Cairo and Addis Ababa in three and a half hours. We did not fly over the Sudan. Numeiri had forbidden Ethiopian planes to land in Sudan or fly in its airspace and, like Sadat, declared his anger towards Mengistu, the enemy of Allah and of Haile Selassie.

We flew over the coast of the Red Sea, then landed in Addis Ababa Airport. The sun was rising, a refreshing coolness in the air, green mountains on all sides, and a clear blue sky.

The people of Ethiopia looked like ancient Egyptians, tall and slim, eyes black and slanted upwards, ringed necks above tall, slender, pole-like bodies. They were as dark brown as the soil of Ethiopia and its black mountains, the blackness of which melted under the stream of rain like liquid gold and rolled down from the peaks, gushing along, splitting the earth and glittering beneath the rays of the sun like a long snake of phosphorous; like the River Nile, carving its way through the desert over millions of years, creating a long, green *wadi*.

Did grandfather Habashi run with the water that fell from the mountains to the *wadi* when he settled in the Delta, in the village of Kufr Tahla? Did the rest of his Ethiopian family remain on the mountains, not to be colonised by anyone and preserving their original features – those of the ancient Egyptians – whilst we Egyptians lost them?

The Ethiopian blood in my body drew me towards the mountains, deep inside me a passion for the strength of them and an attraction for those proud features, carved in rock. Whenever I looked at a child's face, I recalled my own childhood, as if I had been born here in a time I knew nothing about.

I walked in Churchill Street, then found myself in the large square they call Liberation Square, at a popular festival celebrating the revolution; thousands of people gathered together, men, women and children, faces as brown as cocoa, features as sharp as swords, white robes and white turbans, brown hands holding small flags with three colours: red, green and yellow. They sang and danced and beat drums. Above their heads, three huge faces hung as though in the sky: Marx, Engels and Lenin, their pictures as large as the pyramids hanging in the square. The Ethiopians stared at them, not knowing who these three foreigners were. The procession of ministers and ambassadors began, then the car of Mengistu Haile Mariam arrived, a bullet-proof car.

At night I awoke to the sound of bullet shots. I did not know who had hit whom. My Ethiopian friend Almadh was afraid to talk, withdrew into herself and whispered:

– We have laws forbidding us to speak about politics or to visit foreigners in their homes.

I once travelled with her to a conference in Nairobi. As soon as the plane was in the air and had crossed the Ethiopian borders, she sighed deeply, then said:

– I hated Haile Selassie like all Ethiopians. We hoped for a change for the better, but now we even fear words. They speak of Marxist-Leninism in a language none of the people understand. Don't we have national heros and personalities in our own history, whose pictures we can hang in the squares instead of those of Marx, Engels and Lenin? I am for socialism, but I am against the blind imitation of others and the disregard of our own history.

– Tell me about your history, I said to her, and how the revolution against Emperor Haile Selassie happened. All I know about it is that he ruled with the power of Allah, like Sadat in our country. How did the revolution against him succeed?

Almadh told me the story of Haile Selassie. It was like the story of *A Thousand and One Nights*. Haile Selassie was a small, thin man who weighed less than fifty kilogrammes, yet he ruled Ethiopia for over fifty years as an absolute dictator. He regarded himself as head of the church, that he had been appointed as God. But he did not rely on God for his rule, rather on a secret service trained in Europe and America, and on these states' support for him.

It was hard for a small man to have a large standing in a country like Ethiopia were men boast of their height, their strong muscles and their mountainous features. But Haile Selassie he cloaked himself in the personality of the great and raised his head towards the skies. Emotional coldness is the mark of the greatest rulers; emotions in a man are seen as a weak point, the more so for a ruler. His voice, his way of speaking, were so cold it was impossible to judge his reactions. In this respect, he had been completely different from Sadat, for Sadat was extremely excitable. But Haile Selassie regarded excitability as a sort of emotional exposure and kept his emotions unclear. His words too were unclear. Nobody knew exactly what he was saying, for he only moved his lips soundlessly, like the lips of a god, and it was up to his deputy to understand the signs and then convey the message to the people in the form of an order.

His deputy was called the 'minister who transmits orders'.

When things in Ethiopia declined, corruption became widespread and famine prevailed, the people did not imagine Selassie responsible, for a god cannot be at fault. The fault must rather, be that of the 'transmitter of orders'. In every crisis, the minister became the scapegoat. The emperor sacrificed him to placate the people and appointed another minister or a new ministry. In this, he was not very different from Sadat or any other ruler.

Haile Selassie appointed all state employees, from ministers to heads of schools and hotels and liquor stores and bars. In the palace was a special swearing-in hall called the Hall of Hearing where the appointed employee stood bowed before emperor and heard the decision of his appointment. Afterwards, the emperor heard the voice of the employee or of the minister declaring obedience and allegiance and taking the oath. From the Hall of Hearing, the employee moved to another hall called the Room of Naming where the divine bestowal of a title and decorations was made or, on the contrary, where titles and decorations were withdrawn.

Pleasing Haile Selassie meant concentrating on one thing: proving allegiance to him with the movements of the body, standing before him, bowing the head, bending the right knee, muttering some paeon of praise, then moving backwards to the outer door without turning so that no one's back should ever be presented to the emperor's face.

The national income of the empire depended basically on bribery. Every step within a government office had a known bribe. The emperor knew this and realised that abolishing the system of bribery would expose the state to bankruptcy.

Despite his firm belief in Allah, the emperor always feared a conspiracy against him when he was away from Ethiopia. He travelled a lot around the world and loved Europe and America as much as Europe and America loved him. When Italy invaded Ethiopia he escaped to England and returned after some intrepid officers had managed to drive the Italians out. Haile Selassie overthrew these brave officers and took power once more.

He loved travelling and took his jewels and crown with him on each trip, fearful they would be stolen in his absence. He also took with him the men he mistrusted and left behind those he trusted so that none could conspire against him in his absence.

Nevertheless, the number of conspirators against Haile Selassie was growing all the time, and it was impossible for him to take all of them along on his trips. Corruption was rife and discontent widespread extending to the army, the police, and even the emperor's very own guard.

A courageous man named Mengistu Jirmam, head of the emperor's guard, managed to form a 'revolutionary council' consisting of twenty-four officers and during the emperor's journey to Brazil in December 1960, this revolutionary council, under the leadership of Mengistu, deposed Emperor Haile Selassie and formed a new government headed by Haile Selassie's son, Prince Kasa.

The *coup* would have succeeded had the telephone lines between Addis Ababa and the outside been disconnected, but the emperor's supporters managed to contact him in Brazil by telephone and he came flying back. The revolutionaries fled to the forests. Five thousand were imprisoned – Haile Selassie hanged those he could hang and suspended their heads over the doors of his palace.

Haile Selassie resumed his rule of Ethiopia. Privileges and rewards doubled, bribery and corruption doubled. Peasants began to die of hunger, their cattle too.

Famine extended to the peasants' soldier sons and the corpses of soldiers began to appear in the streets. A soldier in Ethiopia did not have the right to be buried where he died, this right being reserved for officers alone.

On 11 September 1974, the emperor heard the sound of demonstrations in the street calling for his hanging. Army men removed him from his palace in an armoured car. When the emperor anxiously inquired where they were taking him, they told him: We're taking you to a place of safety.

A place of safety meant prison. Sadat took this expression from the Ethiopians, Haile Selassie spent twelve months in prison and then died.

Mengistu and his men imprisoned some of the emperor's aides. Some of them escaped abroad, others disguised themselves as monks in the monasteries, some fled into the mountains, returning now and again to Addis Ababa by dead of the night to shoot revolutionaries.

At night, we could hear army cars patrolling the streets in search of Haile Selassie's aides and rebels. Bullet shots echoed through the night.

My house had large glass windows and I could see green mountains from my bed. In the early morning, I would go to the swimming pool at the Hilton Hotel, on the ridge facing Haile Selassie's palace. The water of the swimming pool was hot and steam rose from it; drops of rain fell on my head and I could see both the sun and the moon in the sky. The town of Addis Ababa was still asleep apart from some young people doing weapons' training, rows of men and women training at six o'clock in the morning, the click of their heels on the asphalt, their rhythmic breathing like a silent anthem. In the large square hung the three pictures of Marx, Engels and Lenin, a number of bullets on the chest of each – last night, I had heard shots in my sleep. That morning I learned that some of Haile Selassie's aides had fired at the three pictures in the middle of the night.

The pictures still hung on the posts, resisting the bullets, the downpour of rain and the blaze of the sun. A man born two hundred years ago, who spoke in German four thousand kilometers away, and his picture was still hanging on this Amharic-speaking ridge in the middle of Africa?

The United Nations building faced the square; my office in the economic committee was on the third floor, in the African women's section. The head of the committee had an assistant and the assistant had an Ethiopian secretary. The assistant was from northern Europe, his white skin blotched with red like that of a leper, his secretary was as brown as cocoa. Rumours ran through the huge building of love affairs between secretaries and bosses. The affair usually started on a trip to a conference and ended on another trip to another conference. The conference would be held anywhere in the world other than the boss's country where his wife and children and bank account with its dangerous secret number were.

Ever since I graduated and started working, there had been animosity between myself and my various bosses. Their understanding of management was strange, the relationship between the leader and the led was that of master to slave, absolute obedience to orders without discussion. The leaders in the Egyptian government were pharaohs, but in the United Nations they were holy gods. Silence prevailed in the offices. Employees walked around with light, careful steps and only went into the room of the head or the director with permission. They would knock on the door very gently. If he opened the door, they would not rush in all at once but bit by bit. First the head appeared politely around the door, followed by the shoulder, then the arms and the rest of the body. The last bit to enter would be the feet, advancing slowly and very quietly inside shiny, polished shoes.

At cocktail parties, you would see them milling around the point where the director stood, encircling him from all directions, until they caught his eye and he recognised their faces.

Then they looked happy and they relaxed, as if he had signed his smile in the record of protocol or on the attendance sheet.

My absence at such parties was recorded against me in secret reports. One day the director asked me why I did not come to parties since parties at the United Nations were part of the work. I was surprised, but everyone supported what the director said and regarded my absence from parties as a sort of shortcoming.

There was not much in the town of Addis Ababa. It was a town surrounded by mountains and hostile forces to the north and south. Nothing broke the silence of the day except for the downpour or drizzle of rain or the sound of large carts carrying workers from Addis Ababa to the villages to join in gathering crops. The cars returned loaded with peasants to be recruited into the war or to work with teams of armed people to protect the town or direct the queues of cars at petrol stations, like the queues of people in front of the bakeries in our country and for the chickens at the cooperatives.

At night the silence was broken only by shooting or drum beats that reminded me of the drum beats in my village of Kufr Tahla, the same method, the same tune, the rhythm of feet dancing on Ethiopian soil the same as the rhythm in the Nile Valley. The sound reached my ears as I lay in bed and gave me the feeling that I'd been born here long ago. In front of my house was a small white building with a large courtyard. Men, women and children gathered there, beating drums, dancing and singing all night long. At dawn they disappeared, except if there was a popular procession or festival. Then the whole street would fill with hundreds upon thousands of people carrying flags and banners, shouting in Amharic: Long live justice and equality. Long live human freedom and respect. Down with America and Israel! Some young people carried a large placard on which was written: *We support the Palestinian cause.*

The faces of the Ethiopians were like those of Egyptians, brown and finely featured. Their voices shouting in Amharic were like Arabic voices. When the word 'Palestine' reached my ears, I felt my heart pound under my ribs. I swallowed my tears.

The voices of Ethiopian girls were like song as they shouted 'Palestine' in unison, to the beating of drums. The boys also shouted. Girls held boys' hands and moved forward; row upon row of men, women and children, no barrier or veil between them. Girls raised their heads in pride.

I recalled the recent past when I was on a week's holiday in Cairo and the government had organised a demonstration of public officials in support of Sadat's visit to Israel. Orders were issued from the ministries for the demonstration to go out on two separate days; one for the women, one for the men. I saw women employees on their day walk in the streets in high-heeled shoes, their heads bowed, their eyes lowered to the ground, white or black veils covering their heads. On the men's day, I saw male employees walk in an organised row, their hands behind their backs as though tied by chains, shoulder to shoulder, their backs bowed, looking as if the government had minted them like coin pieces. And like worn out pennies, their features had become faded, almost smoothed flat. Above their heads was a picture of Sadat, in his hand a stick and sceptre, on his teeth pressed the words which he chewed like gum.

Revolution Square was full of Ethiopians from villages and towns. Even men from mountain tribes rode in on the backs of untamed horses, flying through the air like birds of prey, their long, thick hair flying behind them like horsemen of ancient times, their clothes coloured, their horses decorated too; their eyes were sharp as eagles, their movements fast and fleeting as fired arrows or soundless bullets.

Since childhood I have loved popular processions, voices shouting against the English and the king. In primary and secondary school, in medical school and university, in every demonstration I carried a flag and went out. With the peasants I shouted: Freedom, independence, justice and equality.

I swallowed the bitter saliva. There was neither freedom nor justice in my country, neither in the homeland nor in the United Nations.

In Addis Ababa there are many street urchins. I saw them in the streets standing at traffic lights. As soon as a car stopped, they surrounded it holding yellow cloths, shined the windows and asked for money. They chewed *qat* and breathed in petrol fumes as the experts of the United Nations drink whisky and wine. The police patrols picked them up with the garbage when an important visitor was in town and hauled them off to prison. Where they died by the hundred.

The fate of the girl in the street was like that of the boy, unless if she was lucky enough to have an aptitude for immorality: a girl might practise prostitution from the age of ten. There were many kinds of prostitutes – all of them paid taxes and had medical licences guaranteeing them free from venereal diseases. The medical licences were renewed every six months. Most of the prostitutes were young girls who lived in the streets and at night slept in church courtyards or police cells.

Then there were 'kiosk' prostitutes who lived in small straw, corrugated iron or wooden huts. A Coca Cola or soft drink sign hung from the kiosk and in the back room the girl would practise prostitution.

There were prostitutes who owned larger shops, bars or taverns or cafés, and who made money from both trade and prostitution. Each group had a male or female pimp who owned the tavern and gave each prostitute a fixed monthly wage.

Finally there were high-class prostitutes who worked the large hotels or luxury night clubs. The customer would take her home, then return her later to the owner of the place of entertainment. Some of these women had quarters, possessions and influence. Most of the prostitutes were religious. The successful ones did not marry, but an unsuccessful prostitute married because she was poor. A poor prostitute aborted herself by drinking gasolene or petrol whilst a wealthy prostitute did not abort, wanting her child to inherit her wealth.

Most prostitutes were girls who had run away from the countryside. To begin with, they worked as servants, then discovered that prostitution ensured them more money; or they may have been raped by the man of the family, thrown out by the woman and found no other means of livelihood.

In the Joraji tribe, a prostitute would be stoned to death; in the Jala and Tijer tribes, some were punished by imprisonment or beating; in the Amhara tribe, it was rare for a woman to practise prostitution but if she did and if she made a lot of money, she had the same influence as the men of the tribe. In the Burana tribe, women as well as men enjoyed polygamous relationships and prostitution was unknown to the tribe because a man did not pay for a woman, nor was a wife enslaved by a man.

PART ELEVEN

Island
of Slaves

My work at the United Nations entailed continual travelling, to international conferences, regional meetings and development projects in Third World countries, particularly in African ones. On every trip north, east, west or south of Addis Ababa, I flew over Egypt. I found that in order to move from one African country to another, one had to cross a European capital. To reach Senegal or Nigeria or the Ivory Coast from Addis Ababa, one had to fly north to Cairo, then cross the Mediterranean to Paris and from Paris take a plane to Dakar.

For the first time, I realised that our African countries were not yet independent, that there was an invisible rope tying Africa to colonialism. I would transfer from an African plane on African soil to a French or English plane on European soil which then transferred me back to an African plane on African soil. It was like going around the world and around myself to return to the same spot, or somewhere nearby, from which I'd started.

I felt humiliated – our African countries had no contact with each other without the mediation of the colonialist countries. My humiliation grew watching a black African stewardess bow respectfully to everyone with a white skin and jabbering in a foreign language, seeing to their every need with a smile on her face, while when I called her she seemed to be deaf. But the feelings of humiliation dissolved when I was above the clouds, above the land and the mountains, above geography and history, above the borders made by colonialism, and when the plane entered Egyptian airspace, I realised that colonialism did have its uses if I passed through Cairo on every trip.

From the sky I would stare at my homeland and feel my heartbeats under my ribs. My eyes would pierce the clouds looking for solid earth in the enormous melting expanse of the universe. In the darkness, I would glimpse a faint light – the light of my bedside lamp, the bookshelf, my papers, the eyes of my child widening in surprise and fixed on the plane.

But in the streets of Cairo I walked like a foreigner. The picture of Sadat surrounded by light bulbs still hung on walls, occupying the space between land and sky. The earth had turned desert yellow, the greenness of the trees had paled, and the faces of the people were as wan as the earth, their voices choked like slaves.

I took my case and left my small house in al-Giza without washing my face, for my flat was on the fifth floor and the pipes no longer carried the water up. In the limousine to the airport, we crossed al-Giza Bridge. The smell of dead skins emanated from near the graveyards of the new city that they called the City of the Dead, where millions of human beings lived and slept amongst the tombs.

The black Mercedes limousine was luxurious; the new travel agencies worked for high rewards serving foreign tourists. The Egyptian driver wore a cap and spoke into a radio telephone. He took a double fare from me and looked at me in contempt when I spoke in Arabic.

The entrance to the airport was very crowded. One of the entry guards swore at a peasant woman with three children in tow, threw her green passport to the ground and spat, spattering the winged eagle with saliva. I held out the blue passport and muttered some words in English, and he bowed, smiling, and made way for me.

I sat in Cairo Airport staring into space and into my bitter self. I had started speaking English in my own country for my way to be cleared and to gain respect. I felt alienated in my homeland, and outside it I also felt like a stranger. We were still living in the age of slavery.

A sharp sound, a scream or long trill, rang in my ears – an Egyptian girl, wearing a long white wedding dress, had tripped over its train, beads of sweat on her forehead. She walked fearfully towards a Saudi plane, in her pocket a photo of the groom that had come by post, in her father's pocket a bank cheque. From the same plane, the corpse of an Egyptian peasant inside a wooden casket was unloaded, in his pocket a photo of his mother and bundle of *dinars*. The trilling mingled with the sound of mourning and wailing. Rows of Egyptian peasants lay on the airport floor, under their heads a basket or torn suitcase tied with string, on it a name and address in squiggly Arabic.

For the first time in Egypt's history, peasants were emigrating in search of a livelihood. The Sadat years had brought the country foreigners and Israelis, and had expelled nationals, even peasants, who were leaving village lands uncultivated. Foreign companies were turning agricultural land into offices with reinforced cement. Israeli bananas forced Egyptian bananas out of the market; American shampoo flooded in and Nablus soap had vanished. People drowned in sweat running after bread.

The airport seats were now of orange-coloured imported plastic. The airport cleaners wore foreign suits and swept the floor with English lettering on their backs.

I seemed to be in an airport other than Cairo: these men and women workers were not Egyptian but brown-skinned English or Americans. Perhaps Sadat's government had imported men and women to sweep the floor? I began studying the English lettering on the sweepers' backs. My astonishment grew when I learned from one of them that he was not English or American but an Egyptian from Upper Egypt hired by an English company that was in charge of cleaning Cairo Airport.

I could imagine the government appointing a foreign expert in an obscure scientific field or in case of a complex technological problem, but to hire an English company to clean the floor of our airport, that I could not grasp.

This was what Sadat's rule had brought us to: from being well on the way to heavy industrialisation, we had become incapable of sweeping our own airport ourselves, or rather, we swept it with our own hands but under the direction and supervision of the English, as if declaring to all and sundry that we possessed nothing but our arms and always needed a brain other than ours to put us to work and manage us.

I remember a passage I read in a newspaper in November

1977 after Sadat's visit to Israel. It was written by Menachem Begin. In it he said that the good relations which could be established between Egypt and Israel would depend on the benefit each country got from the potential of the other country – Israel had brains and Egypt had brawn and the two should cooperate: Israeli brains and Egyptian muscles would make the universe bloom.

No doubt Begin meant the Israeli universe!

It was strange to see the same sight in Jeddah Airport. There I saw Saudi workers sweeping the airport, on the backs of each a sign in English and American lettering.

It was stranger still that I did not see these signs on the backs of sweepers in Dar es Salaam Airport or Aden or Dakar or New Delhi or Columbia or even Zanzibar, the island of slaves.

The French plane took me from Paris to Dakar. From the air, I looked down on the Straits of Gibraltar. The blonde French stewardess put a tray of food and a glass of wine in front of me, a folder of different kinds of music and pair of headphones which I put to my ears. I turned the knob fixed in the seat and listened to Beethoven and Chopin and Mozart. Twelve different channels brought me twelve sorts of music in the air, from classical symphonies to African Congo dances.

On the screen in front of me, an American film *Love and Crime* was showing shooting, horses leaping over mountains and a black woman being raped.

I slept, then awakened to the sound of the stewardess announcing in French that we were landing in Dakar. Searing sun, dust and the smell of sweat, bodies lying on the ground. A United Nations car took me to a huge hotel overlooking the sea. Around platters of grilled meat and glasses of chilled wine, I sat amongst United Nations experts, a new development project in the pocket of each.

I have watched these international experts since I started working at the United Nations. I did not really know them and the word 'expert' filled me with awe. Then, I was still working for the Egyptian government and if one of these experts came to meet the minister, the whole ministry would be seized with excitement. The tremor was infectious. I sat slunk in my seat before the 'international expert', ears pricked up, fearing to miss a word or a pearl of wisdom that might fall from his lips. I would accuse myself of stupidity if I did not understand something the 'international expert' said or if I did not understand the connection between what he said and the problem of hunger in Egypt or India in which he specialised. And when he did visit Egypt or India, he would stay in the Hilton Hotel or Menna House.

That was until I got the chance to get to know these world experts at their meetings and international conferences. Their sole concern was to solve the problem of hunger for us poor. At every conference I attended, I was astonished at the vast amount of cocktail and supper parties, and such rare enthusiasm for the problem of hunger over platters loaded with food.

I did not go to parties in evening dress like the international experts. My appearance always took the form of a woman of the poor of the Third World; the United Nations experts were surprised and regarded my presence in their midst as something peculiar.

But their talk flowed with concern for poverty and the poor. They did not stop talking about hunger at their meetings and parties and in papers and studies and as soon as they saw a hungry or poor person, they complained. I would sit amongst these experts, watching and listening. Like government employees, they had one style, one way of talking, of moving lips, eyes and hands. Even their briefcases were of the same type, the papers inside of the same form, their resolutions of the same wording.

I used to say that government employees had an excuse since the government minted its employees just as it minted money. But who minted international experts, one a carbon copy of the other?

I realised that international organisations were another government. They could be a government above or under other governments, they could exist as a shadow government, but they did not differ from any other government. One who entered was lost, even if he earned thousands of dollars; one who left was reborn, despite poverty and hunger.

In the luxury Hotel Dakar overlooking the Atlantic Ocean, I

sat amongst these international experts. One of them presented a new development project in Senegal. The budget for the project was 126 thousand dollars divided as follows:

> *First stage, first year:*
> 41 thousand dollars, annual wage of expert
> 20 thousand dollars, annual wage of expert's assistant
> 5 thousand dollars to buy a car for the expert
> 15 thousand dollars, annual wage of expert's chauffeur
> 5 thousand dollars for publishing reports
> 10 thousand dollars for new technological equipment
> *Second stage, second year:*
> 30 thousand dollars for holding a conference in New Year for project follow-up.
> Total: 126 thousand dollars.

I took out of my pocket a United Nations report on the five basic results of development projects in the Third World. I put the report in front of them. The report was summarised as follows:

It is clear from United Nations studies on development projects in Africa, Asia and South America during the period of development, that these projects have failed and that their results were adverse, as follows:
1 – Increasing the gap between First World countries and Third World countries.
2 – Increasing the gap between rich and poor in the same country.
3 – Raising the economic level of United Nations experts.
4 – Lowering of cultural, industrial and agricultural production in the Third World.
5 – Doubling of profits of technological factories in the First World.

The experts put down their glasses of wine, raised their spectacles to their eyes, were sceptical about the validity of the report and asked what the source of the information was.

The source was the United Nations itself. Eyebrows arched in surprise. They put on their glasses again to make sure that the source was really the United Nations, that the emblem was not forged, that the signatures were correct.

They took up their glasses of wine, raised their eyes skyward as if awaiting inspiration or revelation, sipped slowly, then admitted in sad voices that the development projects had really failed, and wondered why.

Suddenly one of them leapt to his feet, his eyes shining with both enthusiasm and wine, and shouted:

– The population explosion!

They all repeated excitedly:

– Yes, the population explosion!

In a calm and quiet voice, one of them stepped onto the platform and said:

– Since the first international United Nations-sponsored conference on population in Bucharest in 1974, the world population rate has only decreased by 0.3 percent, from 2% to 1.7%.

They all breathed a sigh of relief and their muscles relaxed completely.

The expert continued:

– The problem, ladies and gentlemen, is that the fertility of Third World women is increasing, while the land is losing its fertility. According to the calculations of the world bank and the reports of the United Nations, the world population has increased over the last ten years by 770 million, so that today there are 4.75 milliard. This number will double by the year 2025 to 8.3 milliard, of which 7 milliard live in countries of the Third World.

The expert swallowed a piece of grilled chicken leg, then said:

– The failure to control population growth in the Third World will have serious consequences – the spread of hunger and unemployment, environmental pollution, cancerous growth in the cities and an increase in worldwide violence, terrorism and instability. The continuing fertility of women in Africa, Asia and

Latin America will lead us into a world without hope threatened by famine, anarchy and the law of the jungle, a world filled with destructive weapons in the shape of new human mouths demanding food. In Black Africa, women's fertility has increased so that in Kenya, for example, the average number of children is seven. Also, the raising of health standards has led to a lowering of the infant mortality rate. Thus the population of Kenya may grow from 20 million today to 83 million by 2025. In Bangladesh, women's fertility rate, the average number of children she bears in her life, is 6.3 and this means that the population of Bangladesh will reach 266 million in 2025, or three times the present number. The fertility rate in India is 4.7 so that by the year 2025, the population of India will be 1.5 milliard, the birth rate for an American and West European woman, on the other hand, is only 1.6 children. Thus we can see that bad conditions in countries of the Third World lead to an increase in fertility amongst women and that the increase of economic development in these countries is consumed by the mouths produced from the women's wombs, so widening the gap between the income levels of the Third World and the First World. For example, in the period from 1955 until today, the average individual income in America has risen from seven thousand dollars annually to 11,500 dollars, whereas in the Third World, individual income is still between 170 dollars and 260 dollars per year. Thus the gap between the First World and the Third World has increased. The reason is the fertility of women in these backward countries, with the exception of some countries like Thailand and China where the population growth rate has decreased in recent years due to the determination of these countries to implement strict family planning programmes.

The question rang out:

– What do you mean, strict programmes?

An expert whispered:

– The practice of killing girl children in China?

– No, it's the authorisation of abortion, objected an expert.

– No, it's the practice of sterilising men and women without discriminating between the sexes, answered another.

– No, it's neither one nor the other. It means setting up family planning units. In Thailand alone there are four thousand family planning units, said an expert.

– But these units cost a lot of money, objected another. I have a report from the world bank which says that the Third World needs 7.6 milliard dollars in order to set up family planning units.

An expert from America shouted:

– That's an enormous amount. How can we pay 7.6 milliard dollars simply to reduce the fertility rate of Third World women?

An expert from India replied:

– But the world spends 600 milliard dollars on arms every year. Which is more important, the production of arms to kill human beings in war or the production of means to prevent human birth?

An expert from Pakistan said:

– Both of them are murder and that's forbidden by Allah.

An expert responded:

– Better to kill a foetus before it develops in its mother's womb than kill it in war.

Another said:

– Better to prevent sperm entering the woman's womb during sexual contact.

Yet another said:

– That's difficult. It's easier to remove a woman's womb or block the fallopian tubes where the sperm meet the egg.

The expert from America replied:

– Better to prevent polygamy and multiple sexual relations where one man fertilises tens of women.

The expert from Pakistan shouted:

– Allah permits a man to have a number of wives and concubines.

An expert from Sweden asked:

– What does 'concubines' mean?

The Pakistani expert replied:

– It means slavegirls.

The Swedish expert shouted:

– Do you still have slaves? Hasn't slavery been banned since the last century?

An expert from France answered:

– Do you know the basic reason for the population explosion in the Third World?

Everyone shouted:

– What is it?

The French expert replied:

– It's polygamy. I have in my hands a report that says that the birth rate amongst Muslims is higher than any other.

The Pakistani expert was furious and said:

– It's not Islam but the failure of development projects.

The American asked:

– And why do development projects fail?

The Indian replied:

– Because these projects do not meet the needs of Third World countries but those of the First World.

The Swede asked:

– And why don't they meet the needs of the Third World?

The Indian answered:

– Because those who make the projects are First World experts and not Third World experts.

The American asked:

– And you? Aren't you an expert from the Third World.

The Indian replied:

– Yes, but I live with you in New York.

Everyone laughed. The president sitting at the table announced the end of the conference. Everyone agreed to a resolution to hold another conference to discuss the same problem the following summer in the Swiss mountains and agreed to authorise ninety-five thousand dollars for this new conference.

I met a girl called Anne whom I had seen riding a motorbike along the street overlooking the ocean. She had delicate features and dark skin. She was twenty-five years old. Her mother was Senegalese, had married a man from the Ivory Coast, and had seven children by him before he left her. Anne had lived with her mother and siblings, then come to Dakar to work in the press. She had saved up to buy the motorbike, travelled in West Africa and studied the situation of women there.

I went with her to Dakar Museum beside the huge parliament

building, and she took me to a large room in which were statues of African men and women. I noticed one statue of a woman with a large body and head, her smaller husband beside her.

– I saw this tribe in Mali and the Ivory Coast, said Anne. The woman there is stronger than the man and works in the field and in the house. The man is lazy and hardly does anything.

I was reminded of the tribes I had seen in South India where the women worked and provided for the children while the men danced around the god Shiva and adorned themselves with jewellery and make-up.

– My mother was the one who worked and provided for us, said Anne.

We went out into the street and walked towards the ocean. The Senegalese are very attractive, skin the colour of cocoa, gleaming smiles and slim-bodied. Everywhere felt peaceful and secure. Some people spoke Arabic, a group of women prayed in the open air, a man in a mosque called people to afternoon prayer, a small child approached us and asked for a franc.

We arrived at the boat which would take us to Jawriya island. The boat moved off from the Dakar coast and the air grew cool and refreshing. From afar, the island appeared like a rock in the middle of the Atlantic Ocean. Anne sat beside me, her curly black hair done up in tiny plaits close to her head, her pointed nose raised in pride and strength.

– I'll tell you a story I heard from an African woman on the Ivory Coast, she said.

Once upon a time, the great god in the sky wanted someone to help him do something so he called the women. But the women were busy working, tending the land, churning the milk to feed the young, covering huts with mud to keep out the wind. The Lord called to them saying: Come here, I will send you on an important task. The more cowardly women said: Yes, we'll come, but wait a moment until we've finished our work. After a while, the Lord called them again. The women again replied: Wait a moment until we've finish the feeding and roofing the huts. At this time, men did not milk the cows or build huts or go in search of firewood or water as the women did. Their sole work was to put up walls around the houses. Because they had hardly any work, they rushed to answer the Lord's call, saying: Send us, O Father, instead of the women. The Lord went to the women and said: You women will never finish your work, for as soon as one job is done, there's another one. Because they heeded me when I called, the men will have rest, but you women will work and toil without rest till the end of your days.

Since that time, a woman's life has been work and toil and exhaustion. Time passed. A day came when foreign men arrived bringing with them books and pills and guns. The men who were at rest welcomed them and men began to be divided into two parts: leaders who did not work and slaves who worked without a break. The slave was trained to respect work through paying taxes. As for the women, they continued working unnoticed. Finally, the women asked their children, sisters and husbands to compensate them for their efforts. But the men reminded them that the Lord had destined them to be the servants of mankind. They said that the books which the foreigners had brought also confirmed the place of woman as beneath man. Some of the women raged: The greatest obstacle for a person is to be poor and a woman. Other women began to look for ways of liberation.

Anne ended her story and laughed, her white teeth gleaming in her black face, her eyes shining like her teeth. The boat stopped at the island shore and Anne jumped from the boat to the land in one leap, her tall slender body like a dancer's. She walked with head held high, full of confidence and pride.

We climbed to a castle overlooking the ocean and sat on a rock, looking at Senegal in the distance.

– From this island, Anne said, they took my maternal grandmother and sent her to America. This island has a long history: in the fifteenth century the Portuguese and the Spanish began to look for a new way across the seas. The Arabs controlled the way to the east where the wealth was. In 1444, Portuguese ships arrived at this island and soon made it a centre of trade with Africa. At the end of the fifteenth century, the Dutch came, named the island Jawriya and built this fort on the hill and another one on the coast. Despite these two forts, the Portuguese invaded the island in 1659, then the English in 1664.

The mixed descendants of Europe and Africa continued to

live on Jawriya. In 1749 there were only 66 inhabitants on the island, who owned 131 slaves. The number of inhabitants had increased to 2000 by 1786. The French returned in 1789, and King Louis VI appointed ten French rulers over the whole of Senegal. Trade flourished after the discovery of peanut oil, and the island's inhabitants grew to 6000, 4000 of which were African slaves who were only liberated in 1848.

When Anne had concluded the story of the island, we left the castle and went into the slaves' house which had now become a museum.

The upper floor of the house had been for slave-trading whilst the ground floor was divided into rooms – the weighing room was where they put the slaves on scales, as they weighed cattle. If the slave was under sixty kilos, they locked him in the room for a period to fatten him up.

On the room when the women slaves had been kept was written a phrase in French which meant 'A woman's worth is in her breasts'. A woman's breasts would be examined to determine her selling price. Men had their teeth examined. At the bottom of the house was a door leading to the ocean. Slave traders had tied up their slaves with chains and made them walk on wooden planks to the ship. Some of the slaves would throw themselves into the water and a diver would dive in after them and return them to the ship. Twenty million slaves were sent to America. Some say that the number was 200 million.

– Men and women slaves, said Anne, freed themselves. They were not freed by the Europeans, as history states. There was an army of women who fought in the nineteenth century against the colonial army.

We left and walked along the shore to a small restaurant in which a Senegalese band was playing music. The singer was a tall slim youth wearing a coloured shirt. He played an instrument that resembled a lute and sang a popular folk song. I did not understand the words but Anne translated them for me: the song told of a beautiful young girl who on her wedding night was afraid that her groom would discover she was not a virgin, so she had a virgin girl take in her place in the marriage bed. But the groom's family found out and the song ended with the girl's suicide.

– This song, said Anne, is only sung by patriarchal African tribes that enslave the women and circumcise the girls. Matriarchal tribes regard women as people and do not practise clitorodectomy; on the contrary, from the moment a girl is born, the mother or aunt begins to activate the clitoris by massaging it so that it develops and grows bigger and longer.

The Senegalese youth was still playing on his instrument and singing. People gathered round and began to sing and dance with him. Among the dancers was an elderly American woman named Suzi who had been living in a house on the shore of the island for ten years. She later took us to her house to drink tea. In the courtyard of the house was a large tree and in the back room a typewriter on a low table with low chairs like those of Buddhists. Suzi was 75 years old and had been born in Santa Barbara on the west coast of America. She had divorced her husband thirty years earlier.

In the hall of the house, I saw two men sitting on reed mats; a Senegalese man who had lived in America for twenty years and an American man who had lived in Senegal for twenty years. The Senegali spoke English fluently and the American spoke Senegalese fluently. They scrutinised me closely as if preserving my features. The eyes of the elderly American woman sparkled from time to time. There was something mysterious about the house. One moment, it seemed to me like a den of spies, a moment later like a lunatic asylum, yet in another moment the place was enveloped in a rare sort of beauty, the sort of beauty that surrounds a great person with a great message.

I asked the old American woman:

– Why did you leave your country?

– I came here, she said, as a tourist. I fell in love with this island and decided to live out my life here.

She may have been telling the truth. I saw no dishonesty in her eyes, but I do not always believe eyes.

Near Dakar Airport, I sat in the house of Senegalese writer Sembene Othman, a middle-aged man whose hair was turning grey, with black skin and an African-boned body. He held a pipe between his lips; his robe was white and on his feet he wore open sandals. His wife was by his side, tall, large and dark, who spoke English with an American accent. She had been born in America and worked in a bank in Dakar. Sembene Othman spoke French as he did not know English. Their twenty-year-old son sat in the sitting room immersed in watching the colour television or one of the video films.

We talked about African literature and culture.

– I don't agree with Sengour's idea of 'negrism', said Sembene Othman. There isn't one culture that comes from a black skin and another that comes from a white skin. Culture comes from the mind and there is no such thing as a black mind or a white mind. But there are African, Asian, South American peoples who have suffered from colonialism irrespective of the colour of their skins. Besides, Sengour is not the founder of negrism. I am not with Sengour – everything he does is a failure. His politics here are like Sadat's in your country, whereas Abd al-Nasser is loved by all African people.

– That's true, I said.

– Are you a Nasserite? he said.

– No, I said.

– Are you a Marxist? he asked.

– No, I replied. I don't like to label myself. I am for justice, equality and freedom for women, men and country. Abd al-Nasser was great, but he also made great mistakes. Marx was a great thinker, but his ideas are lacking, particularly as regards the situation of women.

– That's natural, Sembene Othman said. There is no final word on anything. I agree with you that the independence of the writer is important, but I chose to be a member of the Senegalese Communist Party, for political struggle through the party is the only way to change the system and we need a change. Many people imagine that Senegal is an independent country because its rulers are black Senegalese men. But these black rulers are more dangerous than others because colonialism hides behind them.

Back to Egypt. I began to think of those black or native rulers in our region who collaborate with colonial power against their people.

Sadat came to power after Nasser's death in September 1970.

I felt that Egypt would suffer under Sadat; unlike Nasser, Sadat was pro-capitalism, pro-America. He encouraged the most backward fundamentalist Islamic right-wing groups to neutralise the Nasser groups and the so-called socialist groups.

As a socialist feminist I had to suffer under Sadat's regime. My books were censored and I was put on the black list. I lost my post at the Ministry of Health in 1972 and had to look for a job outside Egypt. I worked for the United Nations in Beirut and Africa for a while, but then resigned; my boss at the UN, like my boss in the Egyptian government, did not like my independent personality.

I went back to Egypt in 1980. Sadat had already started what he called 'democracy', or a multi-party system, with its opposition newspapers.

I believed Sadat when he spoke about democracy. I published some articles criticising his policy in one of the opposition papers. On the 6 September 1981 the police broke down my door and took me to jail. My one crime was that I had believed Sadat's democracy to be sincere. With me, in the jail, were almost all the opposition leaders in Egypt.

Sadat was assassinated on 6 October 1981 – exactly one month after he had put me in prison. The new president, Mubarak, did not release me for two months after the death of Sadat.

During the 1980s and 1990s I travelled to many countries all over the world. This will be the second part of this book.

I am no longer on the black list. But I am on the so-called *grey list*. I can publish some of my work in Egypt. But the regime is not happy with what I write. I always belong to the opposition. I think most creative writers belong to the opposition in their countries. It is very difficult for creative writers to conform with or obey the ruling regime, especially if it is oppressive. Egyptian government is more democratic than most such regimes. At least I can travel.

Travelling to me is always a relief and a new experience. I have many friends all over the world. We know that almost all governments are oppressive and undemocratic. I have no more illusions about so-called western democracy.